Found in Translation

"Nataly Kelly and Jost Zetzsche have assembled a treasure trove of interesting and entertaining stories to show how translation and interpreting affect all aspects of life. Anyone with an interest in languages—both spoken and signed—will enjoy this book."

—Marlee Matlin, Academy Award–winning actress

"A fascinating book about language and the importance of translation. Kelly and Zetzsche demonstrate how technology and translation help build communities and expand the quest for knowledge on virtually every subject."

—Anthony Salcito, Vice President of Education, Microsoft

"Nataly Kelly and Jost Zetzsche have done essential work in capturing the stories behind translation, and how we all experience its value every day. As they observe, 'Right this very minute, translation is saving lives, perhaps even yours.'"

—Laura I. Gomez, Localization Manager, Twitter

"*Found in Translation* is a meditation, an exposé, and practical guidebook to humanity's continued, painstaking ascent of our monumental tower of Babel. Without language diversity, we would be intellectually impoverished, and with it we are enriched. But without translators to interpret and bridge that diversity, we would remain ignorant and isolated, locked each of us in our own native tongue's limited worldview."

—K. David Harrison, PhD, Swarthmore College
and National Geographic Society

D0180045

"This is by far the most meaningful book on the subject of translation that I have ever seen. The authors have managed to entertain, inform, and show how translation impacts all aspects of our life, from health to business to entertainment and technology, all supported with real-life examples."

—Ghassan Haddad, Director of Internationalization, Facebook

"During times of war, weapons make the difference. During times of peace, battles are won in conference rooms—and those who can most clearly communicate their messages win. *Found in Translation* demonstrates to us all that translation and interpretation are the most intelligent weapons for triumphing in commercial, financial, or diplomatic settings."

—Olga Cosmidou, Director General for Interpretation and Conferences, European Parliament

"Nataly Kelly and Jost Zetzsche focus in on what is the core issue for diplomats, entrepreneurs, non-governmental organizations, and everyday working people alike: language. With information now flowing both globally and instantaneously, translators and interpreters have already ascended into the ranks of the indispensable."

—Sunder Ramaswamy, President and Frederick C. Dirks Professor of International Economics, Monterey Institute of International Studies

FOUND IN TRANSLATION

How Language Shapes Our Lives and Transforms the World

NATALY KELLY
AND JOST ZETZSCHE

A PERIGEE BOOK

A PERIGEE BOOK
Published by the Penguin Group
Penguin Group (USA) Inc.
375 Hudson Street, New York, New York 10014, USA
Penguin Group (Canada), 90 Eglinton Avenue East, Suite 700, Toronto, Ontario M4P 2Y3, Canada
(a division of Pearson Penguin Canada Inc.) • Penguin Books Ltd., 80 Strand, London WC2R 0RL,
England • Penguin Ireland, 25 St. Stephen's Green, Dublin 2, Ireland (a division of Penguin
Books Ltd.) • Penguin Group (Australia), 707 Collins Street, Melbourne, Victoria 3008, Australia
(a division of Pearson Australia Group Pty Ltd.) • Penguin Books India Pvt. Ltd., 11 Community
Centre, Panchsheel Park, New Delhi—110 017, India • Penguin Group (NZ), 67 Apollo Drive,
Rosedale, Auckland 0632, New Zealand (a division of Pearson New Zealand Ltd.) • Penguin Books
(South Africa), Rosebank Office Park, 181 Jan Smuts Avenue, Parktown North 2193, South Africa •
Penguin China, B7 Jiaming Center, 27 East Third Ring Road North, Chaoyang District,
Beijing 100020, China

Penguin Books Ltd., Registered Offices: 80 Strand, London WC2R 0RL, England

While the author has made every effort to provide accurate telephone numbers, Internet addresses, and
other contact information at the time of publication, neither the publisher nor the author assumes any
responsibility for errors, or for changes that occur after publication. Further, the publisher does not have
any control over and does not assume any responsibility for author or third-party websites or their content.

First edition: October 2012

Library of Congress Cataloging-in-Publication Data

Kelly, Nataly, 1975–
Found in translation : how language shapes our lives and transforms the world / Nataly Kelly and
Jost Zetzsche.— 1st ed.
p.   cm.
Includes bibliographical references and index.
ISBN 978-0-399-53797-4
1. Translating and interpreting—Social aspects.   2. Sociolinguistics.   I. Zetzsche, Jost Oliver.   II. Title.
P306.97.S63K45 2012
418'.02—dc23   2012022942

PRINTED IN THE UNITED STATES OF AMERICA

15   14   13   12   11   10   9   8   7   6   5   4

Most Perigee books are available at special quantity discounts for bulk purchases for
sales promotions, premiums, fund-raising, or educational use. Special books, or book
excerpts, can also be created to fit specific needs. For details, write: Special Markets,
Penguin Group (USA) Inc., 375 Hudson Street, New York, New York 10014.

CONTENTS

We dedicate this book to translators
and interpreters everywhere.
Because of you, the world communicates.

Whenever I think about translation, I'm reminded of the movie *Close Encounters of the Third Kind*. The title refers to the three levels of encounter with an unidentified flying object (UFO) proposed by J. Allen Hyneck. Close encounters of the first kind are visual sightings of a UFO. Encounters of the second kind take place when, in addition to these sightings, we see people or objects affected by UFOs. Encounters of the third kind are interactions with UFOs, so that their contents begin to influence our lives and affect our understanding of what it means to be human.

Now replace *UFO* with *translation*. As the authors of this book demonstrate through their vividly presented examples, it's not difficult to have an encounter of the first two kinds. All we have to do is watch translators in action—interpreting for a personality in a television interview, signing an event for a deaf audience, or providing an alternative language on a web page. And we sense the effect of the translation when we note successful outcomes, such as the signing of an international treaty or the completion of a multinational business deal. Equally, we see the effect when a mistranslation causes misunderstanding—a situation that, as the authors show in their anecdotes, can have all kinds of consequences, from the jocularly trivial to the seriously profound.

Few of us, though, take our appreciation of the role of translation to the third level—really grasping how it influences the way we live. "Translation affects every aspect of your life," the authors boldly state on their opening page. *Every* aspect? That's a hugely powerful claim. But by the end of this book you will believe it. You will have seen, in the reading, how multilingual humanity depends on translation for its successful functioning. And you will be impressed, as I was, by the multifarious situations in which—usually without realizing it—the translator's expertise has shaped the way we live. What we find, in *Found in Translation*, is ourselves.

Nataly Kelly and Jost Zetzsche have performed an invaluable service in writing this book. They have not only dealt with translation in a fresh literary way but have made the subject—often presented in abstract and abstruse terms—accessible and entertaining. It is storytelling at its best, with broad themes illustrated by engaging anecdotes and intriguing panels showing how translation enters into the realities of day-to-day living. And the stories, taken from their own experience as professional translators and incorporating a truly remarkable number of visits and interviews, explode some of the myths that surround the subject and bring home to us the enormous problems translators face.

It is the difficulty of achieving high-quality translation that tends to be most underestimated. Language is without doubt the most complex behavior that humans acquire. Typically, dozens of sounds and symbols. Hundreds of syllables. Thousands of grammatical constructions. Hundreds of thousands of words. An uncountable number of contexts in which these linguistic features are used. And all of this done at least twice for most people on the planet—for most of the human race routinely uses at least two of the world's six thousand or so languages. I believe there is no greater intellectual challenge than to build bridges of intelligibility among these languages, but at the same time their individual linguistic and cultural identities need to be respected. The tension between attaining intelligibility while preserving identity is one of the major themes of this book, and it places the translator, whether professional or amateur, at the heart of the task.

The authors begin with a strongly positive affirmation of the role of the translator in our lives, and this tone permeates the book. But a contrasting note appears at the very end, when they quote a negative term they found in a survey of professional attitudes. Asked to characterize the work of translators and interpreters in a single word, one professional said "underappreciated." I'm surprised the word came up only once. As an honorary vice president of the Chartered Institute of Linguists in the UK, I hear it all the time. Translators do so often feel that their skills and relevance are unappreciated or ignored. Well, they can take some reassurance from this book, which will—as its authors hope in the closing words of their "Final Note"—help change all that. I took my cue for this foreword from the science fiction movies they mention at several places, including the *Star Wars* series. *Found in Translation* is aptly subtitled "How Language Shapes Our Lives and Transforms the World." But their title might equally well have been glossed as *The Translator Strikes Back*.

—David Crystal,
author of *How Language Works*

INTRODUCTION

Translation. It's everywhere you look, but seldom seen. This book will help you find it. *Found in Translation* shines a spotlight into the nooks and crannies of everyday life to reveal that translation is right there, hidden just beneath the surface. Worth an estimated $33 billion, translation is the biggest industry that you never knew existed.

Why should you care? Because translation affects every aspect of your life—and we're not just talking about the obvious things, like world politics and global business. Translation affects you personally, too. The books you read. The movies you watch. The food you eat. Your favorite sports team. The opinions you hold dear. The religion you practice. Even your looks and, yes, your love life. Right this very minute, translation is saving lives, perhaps even yours.

Translation affects everything from holy books to hurricane warnings, poetry to Pap smears. It's needed by both the masses and the millionaires. Translation converts the words of dictators and diplomats, princes and pop stars, bus drivers and baseball players. Translation fuels the global economy, prevents wars, and stops the outbreak of disease. From tummy tucks to terrorist threats, it's everywhere.

This book will help you see how the products you use, the freedoms you enjoy, and the pleasures in which you partake are made possible by translation. You'll also get a close-up look at a unique species of human beings who dedicate their lives to searching for the best ways to say things in other languages. As you'll see through-out this book, there are actually two separate groups of these folks—the ones who deal with written words (translators) and those who deal with the spoken kind (interpreters). You're affected by both.

Why are we qualified to help you find translation? First let us appeal to your brain, then to your heart. We have plenty of street cred when it comes to the fields of translation and interpreting. One of us (Jost) is a certified translator for German. The other (Nataly) is a certified court interpreter for Spanish. One of us (Jost) wrote a doctoral dissertation on translation in history. The other (Nataly) was a Fulbright scholar in sociolinguistics. We have forty years of combined translation experience between us, and we are regularly tapped to speak on the topic around the world. That's the boring part, but it gives you a rough synopsis of our credentials.

Now here's the fun part. To help you learn about translation and how it affects you, we hunted for the most beautiful, compelling, and entertaining stories we could find. In laid-back Mountain View, California, we interviewed the modern-day Wizard of Oz for the translation world—the brain behind Google Translate. In the Vegas heat, we visited the luxurious Bellagio, and found ourselves drawn not to the casinos or fountains, but to a Turkish staff member with an account of a magnificent translation blunder. On a brisk day at the United Nations in New York, we met a man whose Arabic mis-interpretation caused the entire General Assembly to roar with ap-plause. And in a quiet suburb of Chicago, on the eve of winter, we sat down for *Kaffee* and *Stollen* in the home of a ninety-one-year-old gentleman who interpreted for Nazi war criminals at the Nurem-berg trials.

That's just the beginning. We talked with designers of bilingual greeting cards at Hallmark, masterminds behind multicultural marketing at Nestlé, and the person who makes sure that millions of non-English-speaking customers for United Airlines can book their flights on the web. We interviewed interpreters who work for clients as diverse as a professional basketball player, an Oscar-winning actress, and the president of the United States (several of them, actually). We even tracked down Dr. Seuss's translator on a hunch that converting the lines "green eggs and ham" and "Sam I am" into another language would surely be enlightening.

Our quest to find translation was not confined within the borders of the United States. Far from it. We interviewed an Inuit in the Arctic, a Māori in New Zealand, and an Arabic translator in Sudan. We saw how translation fueled by mobile technology rescued victims of the earthquake in Haiti, and how it gives power to people involved in revolutions in the Middle East. We chronicled translation on a flight to Iceland, among poets in central London, and on the floor of the European Parliament. We spoke with people who translate *The Simpsons* in Finland, Harlequin romance novels in the Netherlands, and soccer stats in Brazil. We uncovered beautiful anecdotes and timeless truths about religious translation—in Israel and Lebanon alike. Our quest for awe-inspiring translation anecdotes even led us to outer space (think NASA, not alien life forms).

We ventured far beyond just the languages that you might have studied in high school. We located stories about the translation of Shuar, Romani, and Inuktitut. We learned how translation helped bring one language back from the dead (Wampanoag) and helps another keep on ticking (Irish Gaelic). Our sleuthing for the best stories took us backstage at Cirque du Soleil, behind the scenes at Facebook and Twitter, and onto the gold medal platform at the Olympic Games. We dove many centuries into the past to take a look at how translation has shaped history, and we also got a glimpse into the future.

So now, join us as we recount the very best tales of translation, collected after scouring our sources and traveling far and wide. The stories in this book are, of course, only the beginning. After all, this fascinating yet often unseen universe of translation is all around you. This journey will reveal how translation shapes your world. And it will transform your own perspective in the process.

Let the search begin!

Saving Lives and Protecting Rights in Translation

It is said that life and death are under the power of language.

—Hélène Cixous,
French author and philosopher

Lifeline

The phone rings, jolting me to attention. It's almost midnight on a Friday night. I didn't want to work the late shift, but the need for my work never sleeps. Most of the calls I get at this late hour are from emergency dispatchers for police, fire, and ambulance. They often consist of misdials, hang-ups, and other nonemergencies. I've been working since early this morning, and I'm just not in the mood tonight to hear someone complain about a neighbor's television being turned up too loud. But someone has got to take the call. I pick up before it rings a second time.

"Interpreter three nine four zero speaking, how may I help you?" The dispatcher wastes no time with pleasantries. "Find out what's wrong," he barks in English. He didn't ask me to confirm the address, so I assume he must already have police officers headed to the scene. I ask the Spanish speaker how we can help. I wait for a response. Silence. I ask the question again. No answer, but I can hear that there's someone on the line. We wait, but we don't hear any response. It's probably just another child playing with the phone, accidentally dialing 911. I imagine the little guy looking curiously at the phone and pressing the buttons, then staring at it as a voice comes out of the other end. This happens all the time. I turn up the volume on my headset, just in case it might help me pick up the scolding words of a parent in the background.

Then suddenly, I hear a timid female voice speaking so quietly that I can barely make out the words. "*Me va a matar*," she whispers. The tiny hairs on my arm stand up on end. I swiftly render her words into English: "He's going to kill me." Not missing a beat, the dispatcher asks, "Where is he now?" "Outside. I saw him through the window," I state, after listening to the Spanish version. I'm trying to stay calm and focused, but the fear in the caller's voice is not only contagious, but essential to the meaning I have to convey.

For what seems like an eternity (but is probably just a few seconds), I hear only the beeps of the recorded line and the dispatcher clicking away at his keyboard. I feel impatient. He's most likely looking to see how far the nearest police officer is from the scene. "Interpreter, find out where she is." The caller whispers, even more quietly than before, "*En el dormitorio*," she says. "In the bedroom," I interpret quickly. She adds another few words. "Under the bed," I tell the dispatcher. It's impossible to prevent the image from popping into my head. I can see her, holding the phone to her face, lying on the ground in the dark, jammed in between the carpet and box springs. I feel her fear through the phone line.

"Does he have weapons?" asks the dispatcher. My ears and mouth are in a heightened state of awareness now, ready to volley each phrase into English the instant it comes out of her mouth. "Yes, a gun," she whispers. With a tone that's half authority, half reassurance, the dispatcher informs us that an officer is one block away. As I'm repeating this in Spanish, the caller's voice interrupts, barely audible now. In her faintest tone yet, she says, "I can hear him in the hallway." Before I can even finish interpreting the phrase, she says, "He's at the door." As I repeat those words in English, we hear a click. She's gone.

"You can disconnect now, interpreter," the dispatcher states.

This is a true story from Nataly's experience as an interpreter. She never found out what happened to the caller. Thousands of such emergency calls are placed each year, and many of them require interpreters.

The Seventy-Million-Dollar Word

What happens when there is no one to help with translation? The consequences can be life threatening at worst, life altering at best. Even when individuals speak two languages with advanced levels of proficiency, they often fail competency tests for translation and interpreting. Language conversion, whether spoken or written, requires special skills that can take many years to be developed to a professional level.

A poignant example of what can go wrong when a lay bilingual is asked to interpret instead of a trained professional is the case of Willie Ramirez. Back in 1980, the eighteen-year-old was admitted into a Florida hospital. The hospital staff had plenty of people around who spoke Spanish—this was Florida, after all—so finding someone to communicate was not a problem. Finding a professional interpreter, on the other hand, was another matter.

Willie's family members said they thought he was *intoxicado*. This word is an example of what translators often refer to as a "false friend." That is, it doesn't translate the way it appears it might. (A *false friend* is not the same as a *false cognate*. False cognates mean roughly the same thing in two languages but do not come from the same linguistic root. As an example, the German *Ach, so!* and Japanese *Aa, soo* (ああ、そう) both mean "I see," but are unrelated linguistically.)

The first impression of the word *intoxicado* is misleading. It does not mean intoxicated, but unfortunately for Willie, that's how it was interpreted into English by the bilingual staff person who had been roped into interpreting. Due in great part to this misinterpreted word, Willie was diagnosed incorrectly, leading to the wrong course of treatment and, eventually, to quadriplegia.

What does *intoxicado* really mean, and how do you say it in English? Unfortunately, there really isn't a perfect linguistic equivalent. *Intoxicado* refers to a state of poisoning, usually from ingesting something that is toxic to the system. To provide some in-context examples, *intoxicación solar* means "sun poisoning" and *intoxicación por alimentos* means "food poisoning." Which kind of *intoxicación* was Willie's family referring to? They suspected that he had food poisoning because he had eaten an undercooked hamburger.

Without any context, the word *intoxicado* is not easy to render, even for a skilled interpreter or translator. After all, it doesn't sound right in English to say, "He is poisoned," even though that's the literal translation. A professional interpreter, especially in healthcare settings, is trained to clarify whenever there is any ambiguity about what the speaker is trying to convey. A professional would have clarified to find out what type of *intoxicación* they were referring to, if it wasn't already evident from the rest of the conversation. But the average bilingual? Not a chance. They're not trained to think about the nuance of language and how it can affect cross-lingual communication. (As for the correct way to say *intoxicated* in Spanish, the word is *ebrio*.)

Because of the mistake, Ramirez was diagnosed with an intentional drug overdose. He received a malpractice settlement of $71 million. It was later discovered that his symptoms were the result not of food poisoning after all, but of an intracerebral hemorrhage.[1] Because of the amount of the settlement, the word *intoxicado* is sometimes referred to in translation circles as the "seventy-one-million-dollar word." $71 million is a lot of money. Assuming an annual salary of $50,000 per year, it's enough to pay for 1,420 full-time professional staff interpreters—that's probably more interpreters than all the hospitals in the state of Florida have on staff, combined. Unfortunately, history keeps repeating itself. In 2010, a surgeon at a California hospital failed to provide an interpreter to Francisco Torres, a seventy-two-year-old Spanish-speaking patient with a kidney tumor, and the surgeon removed the wrong kidney by mistake.[2] It isn't to say that the same thing couldn't happen in a language-concordant situation (in which both people speak English, for example). It certainly could, but the risk is greater without an interpreter.

In fact, the costs to the entire healthcare system are higher when interpreters are not used. When language barriers are present, medical errors are more common. There are countless reported incidents of doctors ordering unnecessary—and expensive—diagnostic tests instead of simply paying for interpreting services. When patients cannot understand their instructions, they can easily overdose by accident or take medications incorrectly. It's a risky and high-cost business to forego language services.[3]

Patients may say that they understand some English, leading the doctor to believe it's fine to write a prescription in a language the patient may not speak fluently. However, a Spanish speaker who reads the words "take once per day," could easily think they are supposed to take the pill eleven times per day. After all, *once* means "eleven" in Spanish—like *intoxicado*, it's just one of many false friends that can cause horrific consequences.

Embarrassed to Be Embarazada

Many English speakers have the poor habit of adding an "o" or an "a" to English words in the hopes they might be guessing the correct word in Spanish. It's always a source of laughter for Spanish speakers when a male English speaker wants to say, "I'm embarrassed" and ends up saying, *"Estoy embarazado."* The word *embarazada* means pregnant. Saying, *"Estoy embarazado"* implies that one is both pregnant and male. The best way to completely avoid gender confusion? Say *Tengo vergüenza* (which literally means "I have shame") instead.

A Meatpacking Mystery

On a daily basis, interpreters provide services that save the lives of individual patients, but occasionally, their services can affect the health of an entire population. That's the case of Carol Hidalgo, an interpreter at the Mayo Clinic, who helped solve a medical mystery, preventing a public health scare in the process.

In the summer of 2007, Hidalgo paused to speak with a family practitioner, Dr. Richard Schindler, in the hallway. She had noticed that several of the patients she had been interpreting for—all of whom were seen by different doctors—had been complaining of similar symptoms. They had been reporting that their legs were feeling numb and weak. The patients had something else in common, too. They all worked at the same pork-processing plant in Minnesota.[4]

Dr. Schindler tracked down the providers who had treated patients Hidalgo had interpreted for and quickly spotted similarities between the different cases. Within a week of investigating the matter, he learned that Hidalgo's hunch had been correct. There were eleven cases with patients who had the same symptoms.

Calls to the neurologists at the Mayo Clinic followed. Even though the doctors were colleagues, none of them had seen more than one or two cases of individuals with these symptoms. Hidalgo, the interpreter, had worked with several cases and could more easily recognize the pattern.

The major cause for concern was that these employees worked at a meatpacking plant, but the illness did not fit with the typical injuries that pervade the meatpacking industry, such as those that stem from repetitive motion. In the United States, where food is produced and distributed en masse, an illness among workers at a food-processing plant can quickly spread. Health officials take such issues very seriously. At the same time, sending out warnings can create panic among consumers unnecessarily and jeopardize an entire industry.

After researching the matter further, scientists and factory staff pinpointed the source of the symptoms. Workers at the factory had been evacuating skulls and liquefying swine brains using high-pressure compressed air. This procedure resulted in the brains being aerosolized into a fine mist. The workers did not use a face shield, but sometimes (not always) wore eye goggles, so the particles were inhaled and made contact with their skin. Once the foreign particles entered the body, they seemed to attack the patients' nerves and destroy the fatty sheath known as myelin. With the myelin damaged, the nerves were getting injured.

As a result of the discovery, the Minnesota pork-processing plant—and others throughout the country—stopped liquefying swine brains. Some of the workers with milder symptoms were able to resume their normal activities. Those with more severe symptoms needed chronic treatment due to the damage already done to the myelin.

Had Hidalgo not thought to report the pattern she observed as an interpreter, the number of workers whose health was compromised could have easily doubled, tripled, or worse. And while the root of the problem was not actually cause for a public health scare, this example clearly demonstrates that, in the context of global health pandemics, overcoming language barriers can be a matter of life and death.

Medical Interpreters Save Lives—and Money

A 2010 study showed that professional interpreters improved efficiency and throughput in emergency rooms while decreasing the patient's overall length of stay. The reason? When language barriers exist and no interpreters are available, healthcare providers are more likely to order expensive diagnostic tests to determine what is wrong with patients and monitor their care for longer periods than necessary, resulting in excess spending. The same study also found that patients who had professional interpreters were four times more likely to be satisfied than patients who did not.[5]

Out-Translating the Outbreaks

You've probably seen this movie: Doctors with gas masks and hazmat suits staring into microscopes at rapidly reproducing microbes. Somber politicians viewing graphics that illustrate how quickly the rogue virus will spread if not contained. The desperate search for an antibody. It's the ultimate Hollywood fearmongering scenario of mutant microbes taking over the world. And then suddenly, like during the height of the SARS outbreak in 2003 or the swine flu outbreak in 2009, parts of the horror movie script become reality on the nightly news. When such things happen, we use hand sanitizer, purchase face masks, cancel our flights, and huddle close while the threat lasts. But in between these alerts, most of us tend to forget the lurking menaces. After all, there's not much we can do anyway, right?

Well, fortunately not everyone despairs. Behind the scenes, scientists work diligently to prevent epidemics, enabling the public to regain peace of mind. How does translation play a part? In 1997, after the first outbreak of bird flu in Hong Kong, two physicians from the Canadian federal health department had a vision for prevention. They knew that local media sources often reported homegrown epidemics before the national or international media became aware of them. So, they developed a system to automatically monitor that media in real time, look for certain keywords, and send alerts based on the occurrence of those important terms.[6]

This early alert system, called the Global Public Health Intelligence Network (GPHIN), leads to quick detection and response that can help prevent a wider outbreak. The Canadian physicians developed GPHIN in partnership with the World Health Organization (WHO), processing worldwide news sources in French and English to detect local news reports that mention human diseases as well as animal and plant diseases; biological, chemical, and radioactive incidents; and even natural disasters.

There was just one glaring problem with that early concept: They were looking at media sources in only two languages, English and French. Clearly there was a need to include more languages. After all, chances were slim that the local high school English teacher in the Chinese hinterland would take it upon herself to file a report in English on a disease outbreak in her township. So, the GPHIN developers quickly added Arabic, simplified Chinese (the written form of Chinese used in mainland China) and traditional Chinese (the written form used by most of the rest of the Chinese-speaking world), Farsi (Persian), Portuguese, Russian, and Spanish.

Since its official 2004 launch at the United Nations, the GPHIN system has been retrieving news items every fifteen minutes in those nine languages from news aggregators Al Bawaba and Factiva. It translates the articles from those languages into English, and also translates the English articles into the other eight languages. GPHIN's developers soon realized that the daily diet of approximately four thousand original articles with potentially relevant content could be handled only with a mixture of computerized or machine translation and appropriate human oversight. So the developers chose several software programs to automatically translate information in the various language combinations. Once the articles are machine-translated, the system either rejects them as irrelevant, flags them for analysis by humans, or publishes them immediately to alert the worldwide meta-government and government subscribers of a potential threat.

The Canadian system is still working to keep your neighborhood outbreak-free today. As examples of the system's vigilance, both the swine flu and the SARS epidemics were first discovered by GPHIN. In both cases, the alerts launched a process of response and containment that significantly decreased the severity of the outbreaks.

At first, this may sound like a perfect out-of-the-box solution. Once set up, the program operates indefinitely without too much additional work, right? Well, not exactly, say the developers. Algorithms need ongoing fine-tuning to match the constantly changing developments in each language. For instance, the Chinese term for AIDS is 艾滋病 (*aizi bing*). Its first part, *aizi*, is a transliteration for "AIDS," and the second part is a classifier for *disease*. Locals often use unofficial terms, such as 愛滋病, 愛资病, or 爱自病, which are all pronounced identically but also mean "the disease caused by love," "the disease of loving capitalism," or "the disease of loving oneself." The GPHIN system must pick up these unofficial terms and translate them properly too, and that's only possible if it is continuously trained by human specialists.

As another example, take the article titled "Yellow Fever" that was published in the *Tampa Tribune* in 2003. Here's an excerpt: "An epidemic of penalties has thwarted many drives, resulting in a three-game losing streak and essentially leaving the Bucs' season on life support."[7] Ring the alarm bells: There are plenty of terms here to cause the GPHIN system to go into overdrive. However, if the algorithms are smart enough to offset those words with the sports-related terms in the same sentence, the system will not automatically sound an alert. Instead, it hands the report over to a human analyst who can quickly put the information into the right context.

So when you find yourself rolling your eyes at the bizarre automatic translation renderings you find on the web, remember that there are some uses of computerized translation tools that are saving lives. And in the process, translation keeps the hazmat suits and political disaster scenes on the screens of Hollywood and out of our daily lives.

Helping Rescuers in Haiti

While translation helps prevent some disasters, there are others that are harder to foresee. In times of such emergencies, spoken language communication is vital. The ability to say something as simple as "If you hear me, knock three times" in another language can mean the difference between locating a survivor or leaving that person behind—especially someone who is unable to speak due to extreme pain, fatigue, or hunger. Time is of the essence in a relief or recovery situation, but language barriers slow things down. For domestic and international disasters alike, language can make or break rescue efforts. Thankfully, technology is changing the speed and ease with which vital language support can be accessed.

After the earthquake struck Haiti on January 12, 2010, virtually all lines of communication between the affected areas and the rest of the world went down, with one exception: the transmission of SMS, or text messages. The existing emergency response number failed, but Digicel, the largest mobile telecommunications company in the Caribbean, immediately made a free phone number available to a group of organizations that set up an information-sharing platform. Technical solutions for capturing and channeling the thousands of messages were quickly in place, but the majority of the messages were in Haitian Creole, a language unknown to most responders. The relatively few professional translators in the area were already completely overwhelmed by other responses and were unable to handle this onslaught of additional translation tasks.

Enter Rob Munro, a linguist and graduate fellow at Stanford who had been developing methods for processing large volumes of SMS text messages in less-common languages. He'd also been working on crowd-sourcing projects. These two distinct specialties became the perfect combination for a new project called Mission 4636, which was named after the number of the free phone line the individuals used to communicate. Munro went about setting up a team for the task. In the first week alone, he assembled more than a thousand volunteers from a total of forty-nine different countries.

An online chat room served as both the orientation venue for newly joining volunteers and as a platform for translators to communicate with each other and their coordinators. The online collaboration was critical. Many of the messages received were full of colloquialisms that required further discussion, and many translators had specific local knowledge that they needed to share with rescuers on the ground. Mapping data were also embedded, so that translators could apply their local expertise to remotely help responders generate the exact coordinates for a given (written) location and respond appropriately at the scene. Here is an actual text message exchange between translators and rescuers:

M: Hi, Wondering what is "akwatab"? Is this short for potable water? Thanks,

M K: "akwatab" is some kind of pill that you put in water so that it can sanatize [*sic*] it

R: @M—sounds like aquatab—can we have a bit more context to be sure . . . ?[8]

In the first six weeks of this undertaking, more than forty thousand text messages were received, translated, and sent back with an approximate turnaround time of ten minutes or less. One U.S. Marine working on the ground in Haiti described the system's impact like this:

> *I cannot overemphasize to you what the work of [Mission 4636] has provided. It is saving lives every day. There are hundreds of these kinds of [success] stories. The Marine Corps is using your project every second of the day to get aid and assistance to the people that need it most.*[9]

Beginning one month into Mission 4636's one hundred days of operation, the volunteer efforts were gradually transferred to paid workers in Haiti, creating employment opportunities in an area where the earthquake intensified the country's prior scarcity of jobs.

Munro concludes one account of his experience with these words:

> *With far too many people to thank, I will limit the expression of gratitude here to the Haitian population that sent reports. Their selflessness in the face of a crisis of this scale*

is humbling. They shared information not just about emergencies but also any information that they thought would benefit the relief efforts. Despite the tragedies surrounding them, mèsi *(thank you) was among the most frequent words in the reports.*

Munro told us, "As the main responders were the military, most exact cases remain classified. But in unclassified announcements they assured us that it was saving lives every day."[10] The program ran for approximately a hundred days, saving at least that many lives.

The Challenge of Translating Creoles

A creole language is a natural language developed from mixed parent languages. It is established when it is spoken natively by children as their primary language. To better understand how a creole language is formed, it can help to compare the composition of creoles with other languages. According to MIT professor of linguistics Michel DeGraff, Haitian Creole derives 90 percent of its words from French, whereas English, a Germanic language, derives 35 percent of its words from its Germanic ancestors.[11] The millions of speakers of more than eighty creole languages worldwide have struggled to have their languages recognized as "real languages." This disparity often results in fewer resources for the development of the language, for its speakers, and for translators.

Love It or Leave It?

"This is America. Speak English." That's the sentiment of many people who believe that immigrants should not receive any translation or interpreting assistance. "They should learn English, just like my ancestors did." That's another common refrain of many American citizens who weren't around to see how those same ancestors may have struggled to communicate on their arrival in America. Yet America is not exactly unique for its multilingual status. Of the 193 recognized countries in the world, only politically isolated North Korea is considered monolingual.[12]

America has long been a "pull country" for immigrants, and with immigrants come foreign languages. According to the U.S. Census, 18 percent of all U.S. citizens speak a language other than English at home, and the vast majority of these individuals were born abroad.[13] But it isn't just foreign languages that are spoken on American soil. There were approximately a thousand languages spoken in the Americas before the arrival of Europeans. About 250 of these were used in the present territory of the United States. Contrary to popular belief, these languages were not mutually intelligible, but rather were grouped into diverse branches or families.[14]

Today, only eight indigenous languages have significant numbers of speakers. Navajo, an Athabascan language spoken in Arizona, New Mexico, and Utah, has approximately 170,000 speakers. Cree and Ojibwa, both Algic languages, have around 100,000 speakers combined. Cherokee, an Iroquoian language spoken in Oklahoma and North Carolina, has just over 20,000 speakers left. Choctaw, a Muskogean language present in Oklahoma, Mississippi, and Louisiana, has around 10,000 speakers remaining.[15]

For both the foreign-born and for the people whose languages were spoken in America before the United States became a country, language is the key that unlocks the door to basic human rights. In fact, the U.S. federal government has protected individuals' rights to communicate in their native languages since 1965. That's when a federal law was enacted called Title VI of the Civil Rights Act.[16] The law prohibits discrimination on the basis of national origin, which includes the language a person speaks. So if an organization that receives money (even grant funds) from the federal government denies services to someone because they do not speak English, they can be found in violation of the federal law. Also, hundreds of state laws require the same thing, especially in the context of healthcare services. In other words, failing to provide interpreters and translated materials is, in many cases, illegal.

The United States has no official language, and this is by design. Certainly, there were some Founding Fathers who argued for one, but others vehemently opposed this notion.[17] On the whole, the nation's founders believed in tolerance for linguistic, cultural, and religious diversity within the population. Creating an official language would have restricted this tolerance. How so? Language barriers should not prevent people from exercising their basic human rights. Yet all across America, those rights are violated each day.[18]

A Korean woman in the United States who was seeking a restraining order against her husband, who had threatened to kill her, was denied the order by the judge because he claimed he could not understand her testimony (he did not get an interpreter). In Wayne County, New York, a woman who called the police because her husband was attacking her was found guilty of domestic violence herself when the police used her husband as the interpreter. An Oregon man who spoke Mixtec, an indigenous language from Mexico, was released after spending four years in prison before it was discovered that he had not understood the Spanish-speaking interpreter. In Florida, a man accidentally pled guilty to a felony instead of a misdemeanor because of an interpreter error.

In one instance, a doctor used the husband of a female Arabic-speaking patient to interpret for her instead of using one of the professional medical interpreters on staff. When the patient went to the bathroom, she noticed an Arabic-speaking interpreter in the hallway and begged her to interpret for her instead. The reason? The doctor had asked if the woman had any prior pregnancy losses. The woman had, but was afraid to reveal this information in front of her husband because they had taken place before she had met him. When the husband was dismissed and the professional interpreter revealed this information to the doctor, the additional information changed the diagnosis significantly and affected the course of treatment provided.

The notion that all Americans should be encouraged to learn English goes without debate even by the most ardent supporters of language access. After all, English is the language of power and prestige in U.S. society—it's nearly impossible to live the American dream without it. Most immigrants and Native Americans do try to gain proficiency in English, but it takes time to become perfectly fluent, as anyone who has ever tried to learn a foreign language knows all too well. Simply failing to communicate with someone in their native language does not turn them into an English speaker overnight. In short, to deny access to translation and interpreting services not only oppresses human rights and violates laws. As the Founding Fathers pointed out long ago, providing language access is the American way.

When Cultures and Health Care Collide

In late October 1961, a small Red Cross plane landed in Zurich. Twenty-three Tibetan refugees, a mixture of relief and anxiety shadowing their weatherworn faces, stepped into a world that was to become their home. Since that arrival more than half a century ago, Switzerland has provided a new homeland to thousands more political refugees from Tibet.[19]

Surely they felt immediately at ease in the snowcapped Swiss mountains and clear alpine air. But the similarities between the two countries don't stop there. Both countries have struggled to maintain an identity in the shadow of overbearing communist neighbors (the Eastern Bloc in the case of Switzerland; China in the case of Tibet). This common perspective inspired an outreach and compassion among the Swiss hosts for their Tibetan guests that very few other visitors to Switzerland have ever experienced. Indeed, many Tibetans today have embedded themselves so deeply into their Swiss lives that when the Dalai Lama regularly expresses his gratitude for the Swiss hospitality, he also reminds the exiles to study the Tibetan language.[20]

Refugee and immigrant groups pop up all over the world, and many of the places where they are resettled might surprise you. There are sixty thousand Vietnamese in Czech Republic, ninety-five thousand Iranians in Canada, a hundred thousand Iraqis in Sweden, two hundred thousand Kurds in Britain, and nearly seventeen hundred thousand Turkish citizens in Germany, to name a few. The United States hosts many pockets of refugee communities in unexpected places—fifty thousand Somalis in Minnesota, thirty-eight thousand Hmong in Wisconsin, tens of thousands of Iraqis in Detroit, and so on.[21]

Culture is inextricably tied to language, so interpreters often find the greatest challenges in conveying terms that require a deep knowledge of their own or another culture. For example, Hmong in the United States have a significantly higher likelihood of contracting certain kinds of cancer than other population groups, but they traditionally have no word for "cancer" or even "cell." Medical practitioners and linguists at the University of California (UC) at Davis have spearheaded an effort to create a Hmong neologism for cancer, *mob khees xaws*, but interpreters still have to explain relatively simple statements by a physician in great length, especially to newly arrived Hmong. This leads to a variety of problems, including late detection of cancer and the misunderstanding among Hmong immigrants that cancer is closely linked with their new home. As one Hmong leader said, "Cancer is so new that we do not yet have a word for it."[22]

In such cases, interpreters often do far more than bridge language gaps. They enable people from extremely different cultures to understand each other, especially when those individuals come into contact with each other for the very first time.

No Interpreter, No Justice

What happens when an interpreter isn't provided to an accused criminal who needs one to understand court proceedings? The victims are often the ones who suffer most. In 2007, a Liberian refugee living in Maryland was indicted on nine counts of rape and sexual abuse of his nieces, aged seven years and eighteen months. When the courts had trouble finding an interpreter for Vai, the defendant's native language, extensive delays ensued. Eventually, the case was dismissed on the grounds that the defendant's right to a speedy trial had been denied, and he walked free. (He was later deported back to Liberia, but the victims never did get their day in court.)[23]

Shakespeare and Soap Operas in Gaeilge

Irish. You might know it as Gaelic. But in actual fact, there are many types of Gaelic—*Irish* refers to the type that is spoken in Ireland, dating all the way back to the third or fourth century. If you have any Irish ancestors—about thirty-six million Americans do—many of them spoke Irish. In the 1890s, there were nearly half a million people speaking *as Gaeilge* (in Irish) living in the United States, with approximately seventy-five thousand in New York alone.[24]

What's the status of the language today? If you travel to Ireland, you will see the Irish language prominently displayed at the airport, on road signs, and on the exterior of official government buildings. But you might not be aware that there are people scattered all around Ireland who still speak this language today. In total, there are an estimated 1.6 million people in the Republic of Ireland who speak it with varying degrees of fluency.[25] It has official language status in both Ireland and the European Union.

Estimates of the number of fully native speakers of Irish (people who claim it as their mother tongue) fall between forty thousand and eighty thousand people. Any area where Irish is predominantly spoken at home is known as a *Gaeltacht*. Some of the highest concentrations are found in the Gaeltacht regions of Donegal, Mayo,

Galway, Kerry, and Cork. For example, the Donegal Gaeltacht, one of the largest, has a population of more than twenty thousand inhabitants. It's in the Donegal town of Gaoth Dobhair (Gweedore in English) where the famous recording artist Eithne (known as Enya to English speakers) was raised with Irish as her first language.

What may surprise you even more is that Irish has become a language not just for use in quaint villages of the Irish countryside. In an effort to keep the language thriving and to cater to the tens of thousands of people who do still speak Irish at home, this ancient language coexists among modern technologies. Ireland has a radio station, Radió na Gaeltachta, with programming in Irish. In fact, there is even a television station, TG4, which broadcasts exclusively in Irish. Tune into TG4 and you can watch the weather, the international news, talk shows, comedy programs, and even a soap opera in Irish.

A soap opera? That's right. In the vein of *All My Children* or *Days of Our Lives*, the show is called *Ros na Rún*, a clever word play that can either mean "Wood of the Secrets" or "Headland of the Darlings." *Ros na Rún* has approximately 140,000 viewers—more than three or four times the number of native speakers of Irish—who tune in to the show two nights per week, thirty-five weeks out of the year. The majority of viewers rely on English subtitles to understand the plot twists and dialogue.

David McLoughlin has personally subtitled more than two hundred episodes of the show.[26] According to David, many of the most difficult terms to translate are actually swear words, a uniquely rich treasure of the Irish language. But swear words don't always translate easily or directly. For example, the word *cunús* would translate as "pig" in English, but is much more vulgar when used as a swear word in Irish. So the translators have to choose a swear word in English that conveys a similar degree of offensiveness to the listener. Thankfully, and as anyone who has seen an interview with Colin Farrell can attest, the Irish do not exactly lack swear words in English.[27]

Why go to so much trouble to make programs available in Irish? Wouldn't it be easier to just do it in English, given the fact that pretty much all Irish speakers are fluent in English anyway? Here's one compelling reason to keep the language alive. The Irish language has one of the oldest vernacular literatures in Western Europe—only Greek and Latin are older. The earliest Irish poetry dates back to the sixth century; by comparison, the earliest form of French poetry appeared about six hundred years later. The fifteen-hundred-year-old tradition of Irish-language literature remains unbroken to the present day and has had a major impact on literature in other languages, too. In fact, for such a small country, Ireland and its language have made a disproportionate impact on world literature—English literature in particular.

In his *Midsummer Night's Dream*, the spirit Puck is related to the Irish *púca*, which means ghost. In *Romeo and Juliet*, Queen Mab is a nod to Queen Maeve of Celtic tradition, whose name was written as Mab in Old Irish script. In *Coriolanus*, the title character is greeted with "A hundred thousand welcomes," which is an English translation of the typical Irish greeting, *céad míle fáilte*. Shakespeare also borrowed from numerous Irish songs in his plays. For example, the song "Yellow Stockings," which Shakespeare used in *Twelfth Night*, is an Irish song known as *"Cuma, Liom,"* which means "I don't mind." In *Henry V*, Shakespeare even includes the Irish language directly in his dialogue:

> *When as I view your comely grace*
> *Caleno custurame*

> *Your golden hairs, your angel's face,*
> *Caleno custurame*

The phrase *caleno custurame* is not just some nonsense phrase that Shakespeare conjured out of nowhere. It's the name of an Old Irish harp melody called "*Cailín ó cois Stúir mé,*" meaning "girl from the banks of the Suir" (the River Suir is located in Tipperary, Ireland).[28] Indeed, even *King Lear*, regarded to be Shakepeare's finest work, is thought to be based on the older Irish legend, the *Children of Lir*, which tells the tale of a king deprived of what he believes is his rightful ascendancy over his children and peers. In other words, no Irish-language literature would have meant—you guessed it—no Shakespeare, at least, not as we know him.

So what will the fate of this language of such historical importance ultimately be? "Irish is not dying, but evolving with the times," McLoughlin explains. He believes that during the Celtic Tiger years, many Irish people forgot about their culture and what made them unique as a people. "The argument that Irish is a dying language is one of ignorance," McLoughlin points out. "It's no longer the language of fishermen and small farmers in the west of Ireland, but the language of college students, academics, and television personalities," he notes. "People see it as a token of our identity and a reflection of our national spirit. The attitudes of children are much more positive—they see its future and the values associated with it."

Indeed, the Internet has been quietly breathing new life into the Irish language. Google Translate is now available in Irish, and there is an Irish user interface for Facebook. Many Irish language lessons are available on the Internet, and there are even apps for iPhones and iPads. Who would have thought that you could do a video chat via a Skype user interface in a language dating back to the third and fourth century? Well, you can with Irish.

But perhaps the most convincing reason of all to care about the future of languages like Irish is best expressed in a saying from the language itself, "*Tír gan teanga, tír gan anam*," which translates into English as, "A country without a language is a country without a soul." Though the phrase sounds far more eloquent in Irish than in English, we think Shakespeare would approve.

From Abkhaz to Zulu

Which official document holds the Guinness World Record for being the most translated document in the world? The UN Universal Declaration of Human Rights, which has been translated into more than three hundred languages.[29] Given that there are between six thousand and seven thousand languages worldwide, we wouldn't quite call it "universal," but it holds the record for coming closest. (As for the most translated author, Guinness gave that award to Agatha Christie in 2011, at which point there were 6,598 translations of her novels, short stories, and other works on record.[30])

Have Language, Will Travel

Most languages are strongly associated with a specific place in the world, but sometimes the connection between language and territory is not so straightforward. Consider the case of the Roma community. Also known as the Romani, these nomadic people are often referred to as gypsies by outsiders (though within some Roma communities, the term *gypsy* is seen as a derogatory term). The term *Romani* includes at least eight separate linguistic and ethnic branches: Roma, Iberian Kale, Finnish Kale, Welsh Kale, Romanichal, Sinti, Manush, and Romanisæl.[31]

But the Romani are more than just followers of a lifestyle—they are a distinct ethnic group. Their roots date back to northern India and Pakistan in around 1000 CE. Invading forces pushed them from their homeland, starting a forced migration to today's Anatolia in western Turkey. Frightened and harried, they did not take much with them on their journey aside from their language and customs. They stayed in Anatolia for a couple hundred years, but when yet another invading force arrived, they began moving again. The family groups fragmented, dispersed, and moved over various routes into Europe. They were expelled (or enslaved) at every destination, so whenever they could escape, they kept moving. Although there are no written records of this history, linguists have painstakingly deconstructed the different Romani dialects, identifying commonalities, and relating them to languages spoken in the areas of assumed origin to arrive at this account of Romani history.[32]

With ten to twelve million Romani worldwide, only two million are reported to speak one of the many forms of the Romani language. This discrepancy prompted Debbie Folaron of Concordia University in Montreal to initiate the Translation Romani project (www.translationromani.net), a website and community designed to provide "a language-centric point of belonging." Though it may not be immediately apparent to the outsider, translation plays a crucial role for Romani. Romani visitors "get it right away when they see it," Debbie explains.[33]

More often than not, if a Romani person in Hungary or Russia wants to know what's happening with the Romani community in Canada or Spain, this can happen only through translation. Even if both have maintained some form of Romani, the differences between the dialects can be enormous. Of course, this presents a language problem, even within the website itself. Debbie and her team chose Kalderash, a branch of the Roma subgroup that represents the most widely spoken dialect and is typically used in international forums. Ron Lee, a widely respected speaker and writer from the Kalderash group and the author of the only comprehensive English–Kalderash dictionary, translated the site content. It is also translated into Portuguese, French, Spanish, German, Hungarian, Italian, Turkish, and Czech, all languages spoken by large Romani populations.

Translation Romani provides a virtual home for Romani translators scattered around the world. Romani translators are often not part of the professional translation community. This site provides tools to equip them as professional translators and to build up a professional community by networking with other Romani colleagues. Much more important, sites like this may help a fragmented ethnic group find a territory they can claim as their own, even if it's only a virtual one.

Life After Death

Did you know that translation can bring an extinct language back to life? Allow us to invoke the story of Wampanoag (Wôpanâak), a language that was spoken by Native Americans back when the Pilgrims landed at Plymouth. Ironically, many Americans celebrate the Wampanoag each year at Thanksgiving without even realizing that the group's descendants still live on their ancestral homelands in southeastern Massachusetts. Several words made their way into English thanks to Wampanoag, such as pumpkin (*pôhpukun*), moccasin (*mahkus*), and skunk (*sukôk*). But unfortunately, the beautiful language of the native people who reportedly saved the Pilgrims from starvation faded away. The last fluent speakers died out in the mid-nineteenth century.

And yet, after 150 years of lying dormant, it's spoken every day by members of the Wampanoag community and, most important, by children. This is thanks to a remarkable and determined woman by the name of Jessie Little Doe Baird, who set out on a mission to reclaim the language or, as she says, "to bring the language home." Jessie's daughter was the first native speaker of Wampanoag in six generations.

In great part, the language could be revived because of the existence of a large number of written texts in Wampanoag with corresponding translations in English. The Wampanoag were the first Native Americans to adopt an alphabetic writing system, which meant that they left behind many seventeenth- and eighteenth-century legal documents. Most of these were deeds and wills for which translations into English had been produced while native speakers were still alive.

Another important resource was a Wampanoag translation of the Bible. This enabled Baird to reconstruct a grammar and a sizable dictionary. Anne Makepeace, who made a documentary about the Wampanoag called *We Still Live Here: Âs Nutayuneân*, observes, "The great irony in their story, of course, is that the key to bringing it back, their Rosetta Stone, is a Bible that was translated into Wampanoag and published at Harvard in 1663 to convert New England Indians to Christianity and force them to give up their traditional ways, including their language."[34]

While it took centuries for the language to fade out, the act of reviving it came only recently. The tribes of the Wampanoag Nation started the collaborative Wôpanâak Language Reclamation Project in 1993. To take the project further, Baird applied for a research fellowship in 1996 at the Massachusetts Institute of Technology (MIT), where she worked with renowned scholars in languages of the same linguistic branch (Algonquian).

Of course, translation isn't the only tool that the Wampanoag could use to revive their language. Jessie tapped into the work of other Algonquian languages as well as the Wampanoag corpus to reconstruct the grammar and build a dictionary and pedagogical materials for the language. After two decades of devoting her life to this cause, she has succeeded not only in revitalizing a language but enabling her people to more fully appreciate their heritage. Baird, whose unprecedented work was recognized with a prestigious Mac-Arthur Fellowship (or Genius Grant) in 2010, now aims to launch an immersion school for kids to start learning all subjects in Wampanoag starting from kindergarten.

MIT linguist Noam Chomsky helps put the revival efforts into context in a comment in *We Still Live Here*. He rightly states, "A language is not just words. It's a culture, a tradition, a unification of a community, a whole history that creates what a community is. It's all embodied in a language."

Till Death Do Us Part

Estimates vary as to how many languages exist. The number lies somewhere between six and seven thousand, depending on how one distinguishes between a language and a dialect. This number is by no means stable. According to linguist David Crystal, about three thousand languages will die within the next hundred years.[35] That's about one language every two weeks. (A language is considered dead when the last speaker dies.) Why are efforts made to preserve languages? Because every language is a unique representation of the human experience, and every extinguished language makes humanity that much poorer.

Surfing like a Shaman

Canada is an officially bilingual country: English and French enjoy "equality of status and equal rights and privileges . . . In all institutions of the Parliament and Government of Canada."[36] In practice, this means a lot of translation.

In fact, Donald Barabé of the Canadian government Translation Bureau told us that the bureau billed federal government departments and agencies $171.7 million (Canadian) for translation in the 2010–2011 fiscal year alone, almost all of which is spent on French–English translation.[37]

On the provincial and territorial level in Canada, though, the language landscape looks quite different. It is interesting that there is only one officially bilingual province, and it's not the one you might think because *le français est la seule langue officielle du Québec* (French is the only official language of Quebec). Instead, it might surprise you to learn that it's actually New Brunswick on Canada's east coast.

In the northern territory of Nunavut, most translation efforts are centered around the Inuktitut language. And there's a good reason for that emphasis: In the 2006 census, close to 83 percent of Nunavut's population reported Inuktitut as its mother tongue.[38] Inuktitut (and Inuinnaqtun, a variant spelled with Roman letters) is the name given to the different variations of the language spoken by the Inuit people, who used to be called Eskimos. The Office of the Languages Commissioner in Nunavut's capital of Iqaluit (which calls itself "Canada's coolest arctic city") provides a number of essential translation resources, including this mouthful: the *Inuit Uqausinginnik Taiguusiliuqtiit* (written in the wonderfully strange syllabary as ᐃᓄᐃᑦ ᐅᖃᐅᓯᖏᓐᓄᑦ ᑕᐃᒍᓯᓕᐅᖅᑏᑦ). The *taiguusiliuqtiit* is the language authority that standardizes the Inuit language, aiding translators as they coin new Inuktitut terms for many modern concepts and attempting to provide unity for the vast dialectal differences within the language.[39]

Julia Demcheson, an English-into-Inuktitut translator, provided us with some fascinating examples of this dialectical variety:

> Qujana *means "forget it" in south Baffin, but it means "thank you" in Greenlandic. In some areas of the Baffin region, "thank you" is* qujannamiik *or* nakurmiik, *depending on the community, and in Nunavik—the dialect spoken in northern Quebec—it is* nakurami *or* nakurmiik. *In the Qitirmiut region, "thank you" is* koana, *and in the Kivalliq dialect it's* matna.[40]

It seems that the well-known story of the fifty different words for *snow* in Eskimo languages should have been referring to "thank you"![41]

Julia also highlighted an example of coining new terms on the basis of a rich native heritage that would make any translator's heart pound with excitement. Eva Aariak, Nunavut's former languages commissioner (and later premier of Nunavut), chose the word ᐃᑭᐊᖅᑭᕕᒃ (*ikiaqqivik*) as the Inuktitut translation for "Internet." It's a traditional term that means "traveling through layers," and it refers to what a shaman does when he travels across time and space to find out about living or deceased relatives, "similar to how the net is used now," Julia adds. We can't think of a better example of how the variety of languages and translation can enrich our collective worldview.

And this brings us back to human rights. In its 1996 report, the Royal Commission on Aboriginal Peoples in Canada stated that the "revitalization of traditional languages is a key component in the creation of healthy individuals and communities."[42] Though this has a lofty ring to it, it might sound just a little too theoretical. But consider the translation of "Internet" into Inuktitut and how it can affect your perception of your own world. An additional finding in the same report seems more concrete: "The threat of their languages disappearing means that Aboriginal people's distinctive world view, the wisdom of their ancestors and their ways of being human could vanish as well."

Languages, translation, and human rights: Suddenly it's not only about them, but about all of us.

CHAPTER 2

Waging War and Keeping the Peace in Translation

War is what happens when language fails.

—Margaret Atwood,
Canadian novelist and activist

High-Stakes Interpreting at Nuremberg

I knew there was something different about us, even as early as five years old. I had no grandparents, aunts, uncles, or cousins. The other children would say, "Oh, you're German. You're a Nazi." I felt a deep sorrow, a great loss. I felt like a stranger in a strange land. It trickles down to the next generation, this profound grief and anger over the enslavement and murder.[1]

It was true—at least in part. There was something that made little Nettie and her sisters stand out from the rest of the children in her Chicago neighborhood. She was German, and her family did have a connection to the Nazis—just not the one that kids teased her about in the school yard. Nettie's father, Peter Less, was instrumental in bringing Nazi war criminals to justice (in the legal sense, at least).

As an interpreter for the Nuremberg trials, the international war tribunals organized by the Americans, British, and French, he interpreted for all twenty-four of the captured leaders of Nazi Germany.

But what is remarkable about Peter is not just that he enabled this pivotal moment in human history to actually happen. What is nearly incomprehensible is that the men whose voices he embodied— day after day for ten months—were responsible for the death of his mother. And his father. And his grandmother. And his only sister. Peter's entire family was killed at Auschwitz. He gave their murderers a voice in court, standing mere feet away from them as he did so.

How did he do it? "You have to leave your feelings at home and become a machine," Peter explains. "Otherwise you cannot function; you cannot do what you're hired to do."[2] Peter's ability to control his emotions enabled him to play a critical role in the unfolding of world history. He interpreted at the trials of Hermann Göring and Rudolph Hess, among others. When asked how he could stand to be in the presence of these men, Peter explained, "It wasn't easy. You were sitting in the same room with the people who probably killed your parents, but you could not let your feelings interfere with your job. You swore to interpret as faithfully as possible, to put the speaker's idea into the listener's head. So we did." Less was only twenty-five years old at the time.[3]

But the emotional damage hit deeply. Many interpreters were so distraught that they were unable to continue interpreting. While others had to step down from their posts entirely, Peter remarkably approached his task with an undeterred view of the Nazi war criminals as human beings: "These were still people. In fact, they were extremely intelligent. It would be a dangerous mistake to make them sound as if they were not." Often Peter doubted whether they really needed him to interpret at all. "They understood English, but it was an advantage for them to wait for the translation, to give them time to think and answer."

However, Peter explains that the work was easier for him because of one major factor—as a native of Germany, he understood the culture. "I had a big advantage, because I knew Germans. I knew the way Germans think, the psyche, which is more than just the language. I knew how their mind works."

But Less also had to know how the equipment worked. This was no small task. The method of interpreting that was to be used—simultaneous interpreting—required interpreters to listen and speak simultaneously. For this purpose, there was a new technology being used at Nuremberg.[4] Luckily, Less had attended the École d'Interprètes, a Rockefeller-funded department at the University of Geneva that pioneered the new technology and simultaneous interpreting techniques. Less's class graduated shortly after the end of World War II. One day, some American military officers arrived at the school and tested a dozen people. They hired three, including Less. The next morning, he flew to Nuremberg.

Nowadays, it is well known that interpreters who interpret such harrowing material are likely to experience vicarious trauma. Interpreters who work at international war crimes tribunals are more likely to receive psychological support. No such aid was provided to the interpreters who served at Nuremberg. Psychology was not yet widespread, with Freud just having died in 1939.

In spite of the gruesome content that Less found himself interpreting, he speaks calmly and humbly about his experience at Nuremberg. He even smiles when recollecting a misunderstanding that he jokingly says "nearly led to World War III." The incident seems innocent enough. Less merely interpreted the words, "What did Russia do?" However, Less knew he had made a serious mistake when a Russian officer immediately jumped up and started to wave his hands in the air. The sentence that had actually been spoken at the trial? "What did Rascher do?"

The sentence had referred to the German General Rascher instead of Russia. Less had simply misheard the sentence. It's pretty easy to understand how that could happen for someone listening and speaking in two languages at the same time, under such tremendous pressure, pioneering a groundbreaking technology (one that is still used today) and working in his first real assignment after graduation. It was also his last. With the work he did at Nuremberg, he interpreted enough for a lifetime—indeed, for several—including the loved ones whose lives were lost at the hands of those for whom he interpreted.

We Will Outlast You

You're most likely familiar with the heartless phrase allegedly uttered by Soviet Premier Nikita Khrushchev in 1956, when discussing the advantages of communism over capitalism: "We will bury you!" The problem? That was a literal translation that did not convey the true intended meaning. He was using an old Russian saying—*"Мы вас похороним!"*—which means something like, "We'll be here even when you're dead and gone," essentially conveying his belief that communism would outlast capitalism. Americans took the remark to mean that the Russians wanted to bury them with a nuclear attack.

Art Imitates Death

> **KEV:** (to man) SIR? I need you DOWN on the GROUND!
> DOWN on the GROUND!
> **MUSA:** انتة تحتاج تنزل لل....
> **KEV:** Wait, what are you telling him?
> **MUSA:** What?
> **WOMAN:** مآو شي الكم اهنا! روحوا!
> **MUSA:** I'm telling him what you said!
> **KEV:** What the f***?
> **MUSA:** I'm TRANSLATING!

Of the approximate 1.6 billion English hits found for the keyword *theater* in a Google search in early 2012, 700 million also contained the keyword *war*. The use of the term *theater of war* goes back all the way to the early eighteenth century, when European nobility watched and discussed wars (with great personal detachment) as choreographed events. It was made popular by the German military theorist Carl von Clausewitz in the early nineteenth century as *Kriegstheater*, and it has since been adopted in various languages (*théâtre militaire* in French, *teatr działań wojennych* in Polish, and so on).

To the attentive listener or reader, this term might sound like a euphemistic way of describing the terrible staging of events of war. For some playwrights, however, it has provided tremendous opportunities to exercise artistic commentary on the theater of war through theater of a very different kind. Rajiv Joseph's *Bengal Tiger at the Baghdad Zoo*, which was nominated for three Tony awards in

2011 and cast Oscar-winner Robin Williams as one of the central characters, is one such example.[5]

Bengal Tiger, which contains the dialogue at the start of this section, takes place in the harrowing maelstrom of the Iraq War. But at its heart, it is a play about translation and interpretation on all levels: between Iraqis and two U.S. soldiers through an Iraqi interpreter; between the world of the living and the dead; and between the English-speaking audience and many actors who speak in Iraqi Arabic, which becomes intelligible only as it's interpreted for other characters in the play.

Communication plays as much a role in conflict as confrontation. When conflicts occur between people of different nationalities, ethnic groups, religions, and languages, translators and interpreters become indispensable. But exactly how much do these actors in the theater of war rely on their interpreters? When war breaks out and violence escalates, the dynamic between interpreter and client can change in an instant. More often than not, the bond strengthens. These examples form a larger pattern that tells a similar story:

- *"The interpreter saved my life."*
  —Ian Martin, a British soldier whose death had been ordered by an Afghan warlord

- *"Your interpreter is way more important than your weapon."*
  —Cory Schulz, U.S. Army major embedded with Afghan troops

- *"It cannot be overstated just how crucially important a role interpreters play, and I owe my life to him."*
  —Nathan Bradley, U.S. Army officer who served in Afghanistan

- *"Jacob [the interpreter] may have been the last soldier I was introduced to, but I quickly learned he was the most important."*
  —Captain Tim Hsia, U.S. Army active duty infantry

- *"At every interface between civilian and foreigner in any overseas war, success is determined by the fallible but indispensable software supplied by the interpreter."*
  —Michael Griffin, researcher and author[6]

And what do these interpreters receive in exchange for their courage? An even greater risk of death than the soldiers themselves. In Iraq, interpreters were ten times more likely to be killed than were U.S. troops.[7]

Traduttore, Tradito

Why are interpreters so much more likely than soldiers to die in times of war? The answer can be summed up as follows: *traduttore, traditore.* The old Italian expression, meaning "translator, traitor," exists for a reason. When someone navigates between two worlds, they're often viewed with suspicion by one side or the other—or worse yet, by both sides.[8]

One of the core tenets of interpreting is to maintain neutrality. But how can you remain neutral when some of the people you're interpreting for are trying to kill you, while others are trying to save your life? Obviously, your loyalties will lie with the people who are good to you. But what defines *good*? What if the group that is paying you to interpret bombed a village where your grandmother lived, killing her in the process? On the other hand, the rebels they are fighting captured, tortured, and killed your sister. Where does your allegiance ultimately lie? In many cases, it lies with the ability to earn a living and feed your immediate family. For people living in combat zones, interpreting offers a source of income that is worth the risk—that is, at least temporarily and as long as they have the protection of the troops they are interpreting for. But that fades away when the troops withdraw and the interpreters are left behind.

While the soldiers return to safety and the company of their loved ones, the interpreters rise to the top of the target list for assassination in their home country. They must deal with death threats and often do anything they can to find safety or flee the country. Many cannot even return to their families for fear that their loved ones will be targeted too. Indeed, many of their families are murdered along with the interpreters because they are viewed in the same light, as traitors. It's a heartbreaking reality of the devastation and destruction left behind by armed conflict.

If you're tempted to think that this scenario doesn't happen all that often, we're sorry to bear even more bad news. During the Iraq War, thousands of Iraqis worked as interpreters for the U.S. military. The Department of Defense stated that in a single quarter alone in 2007, there were 5,490 Iraqis working as interpreters for the Multi-National Force—Iraq.[9] And what about Afghanistan? Once again, thousands of interpreters assisted U.S. troops in that war as well. No one knows exactly how many interpreters worked in both wars. Accurate numbers of interpreters who died in battle are also difficult to obtain, but most sources agree that at least three to four hundred interpreters were killed in Iraq, and at least a hundred in Afghanistan.

Is anyone protecting all the Iraqi and Afghani interpreters who have protected American troops and whose lives are still being threatened? In 2007, President Obama acknowledged that "the Iraqis who stood with America—the interpreters, embassy workers, and subcontractors—are being targeted for assassination."[10] He also said that the United States had a "moral obligation" to protect them. Shortly after that pronouncement, in 2008, the U.S. government created an immigrant visa program for Iraqi and Afghan nationals who served American forces as interpreters.[11] Under the program, a certain number of visas were permitted each year. A total of five hundred such visas were available in 2008. However, in 2009, the number dropped drastically to just fifty visas per year.

By comparison, in 2009, tiny Denmark granted asylum to 120 Iraqi interpreters who worked for Danish troops in Iraq, as well as their families.[12] In 2011, the Canadian government announced that it would issue 550 visas for Afghan interpreters who had served Canadian troops.[13] As of 2011, Australia had resettled 557 Iraqis who had supported its military operations.[14]

What will be the fate of those thousands upon thousands of interpreters who risked their lives for American troops and continue to live in fear of assassination? They are likely uttering a phrase with a slightly different spin on the old Italian adage: *traduttore, tradito* (translator, betrayed).

Voice of the Victims

The horrors of any war are difficult to fathom, but perhaps none in recent memory have left the world as heartbroken as the graphic images of the horrific slaughter of human beings that took place in Darfur, a region in western Sudan, from 2003 to 2009. Daoud Hari made sure that you learned about it. At great personal risk, Hari interpreted for journalists from the BBC, *New York Times*, and NBC so that the world would know what was happening to his people.

Hari worked as an interpreter between 2003 and his arrest in 2006. During those three years, he witnessed the murder of his beloved brother, the eradication of entire villages, the debilitating effects of gang-rape on young girls, the mutilation of children, and the violent dismantling of an age-old social structure between the different ethnic groups of Darfur. But instead of carrying a gun to fight these diabolical injustices, Hari used his proficiency in Arabic, English, and his native language Zaghawa to help journalists and nongovernmental organization (NGO) representatives see the atrocities in Sudan firsthand. Those journalists, in turn, reported the stories in their countries, raised public awareness, and increased foreign pressure on the Sudanese government. In the process, he gave a voice to the victims:

> *The stories came pouring out, and often they were set before us slowly and quietly like tea. These slow stories were told with understatement that made my eyes and voice fill as I translated; for when people seem to have no emotion remaining for such stories, your own heart must supply it.*

It's ironic and simultaneously revealing that his autobiography is called the *Translator: A Tribesman's Memoir of Darfur*.[15] Not only does Hari never translate written words—he interprets spoken ones—but very little is explicitly said in the book about the actual process of interpreting. But the appropriateness of the book's title goes deeper than the straightforward dictionary definitions of *translation* and *interpretation*. *Translation* comes from the Latin word *translatus*, which means "to carry over," as across a river, or, in Hari's case, in the form of building relationships. Hari's interpreting skill in orally transferring language between Arabic or Zaghawa and English enabled his employers to communicate within Darfur, but it was his relationship-building skills that allowed them to survive. Only during his final trip, when he was captured by his own Sudanese government and imprisoned under unspeakable conditions, did it take relationships beyond his own to save his life. Hari, the journalist, and his driver were imprisoned and tortured over a period of several months until international pressure made the Sudanese government release the prisoners.

Hari's efforts played a significant role in assembling the testimony of foreign observers that would indict Sudan's president Omar al-Bashir in 2010 in the International Court of Justice and help forge a peace accord in Sudan. At many points in those three years of horror, Hari was given the choice to give up or to fight. He chose the latter, with a weapon that resonated louder than guns: language.

When we think of interpreting, we may tend to picture a UN interpreter standing behind a foreign dignitary and whispering in her ear, a conference interpreter in his booth, or a medical or legal interpreter in a hospital or a courtroom. But the many anonymous military interpreters in the field today surely carry a much heavier linguistic and emotional burden than their colleagues in more peaceful environments will ever know.[16]

America's Language Problem

"Tomorrow is zero hour."
"The match is about to begin."

Al-Qaeda operatives issued these words in a communication on September 10, 2001. The messages, spoken in Arabic on taped phone conversations, were intercepted successfully by U.S. intelligence on the same day. Unfortunately, they were not translated until September 12, the day *after* the terrorist attacks.[17]

Obviously, messages such as these go through a process of qualification before they are considered a credible threat. So it would be an overstatement to blame the 9/11 attacks entirely on a lack of translation. Or would it? It is a well-known fact that the government struggled with enormous backlogs of in-language documents awaiting translation. For example, from 2006 to 2008, the CIA collected forty-six million files but left one third of these untouched, due in great part to the lack of translation resources.[18]

In the years that followed 9/11, the U.S. government made many attempts to correct America's increasingly visible language problem. It issued numerous multibillion-dollar contracts to defense contractors who provided interpreters and translators in places like Guantanamo, Iraq, and Afghanistan. It spent enormous sums to improve multilingual intelligence gathering in languages that were deemed critical for intelligence and defense purposes.

Most agencies that fall under the Department of Defense (DOD) launched exhaustive campaigns to recruit the necessary linguistic resources. The United States invested in better technologies to improve data mining and translate information automatically. Various agencies issued large contracts for services like multilingual media monitoring, and suddenly major contractors in the DC area began hiring full-time language staff for languages like Arabic, Pashto, and Kurdish. The sole job of these individuals is to scan news items and listen to local radio reports in other languages and produce English-language summaries of what is happening on the ground. But all of these efforts were insufficient. Government reports continue to show that America is far behind its optimal levels of linguistic preparedness. Why?

First, American students are not exactly known for their passion for foreign language studies. Add to that a lack of investment in foreign language learning by the government over the past few decades, and what do you get? A major shortage of people with proficiency in critical languages. Of course, some university programs teach foreign languages that are needed by the U.S. government, but there are not enough to produce the numbers of graduates required.

When it comes to linguistic preparedness, one saving grace of the United States could be its linguistic diversity. After all, one out of five people speaks a language other than English at home. Many of these individuals speak exactly the same languages that the government needs, and some are even refugees from places of military importance, like Afghanistan and Iraq. But many of them are not proficient enough in both languages (especially English) to carry out the kind of high-level tasks required for most full-time government translation positions. In other words, even if immigrants and refugees help address the lack of people proficient in critical languages, their lack of English proficiency is often a barrier.

When candidates do have good language skills, though, there's another problem preventing the government from hiring some of them: the image problem. Not everyone wants to work for the

FBI or the CIA. Some see it as morally ambiguous work, especially if they'll be doing things like, say, listening to wiretapped conversations of people living in their home country. Even native-born Americans who study languages abroad often develop close relationships with individuals in those countries that may make them ambivalent about collaborating with the U.S. government's intelligence activities.

And there is yet another major barrier in the way. Many of the translation tasks that are carried out by government employees require the highest-level security clearances. This leaves a tiny pool of candidates. What's more, government contractors receive billions of dollars from Uncle Sam to do all kinds of different language-related tasks that require lower-level clearances. They also happen to pay more. What can be done? Secretary of Defense Leon Panetta has been an advocate for foreign-language training throughout his career, dating back to the Carter administration. However, while Panetta's support for language training is crucial, that alone will not fill the gaping language chasm facing the United States. It takes years to become fully fluent in a foreign language. Simply investing more in foreign language education might have worked for America back in cold war times, but not anymore.

There are several things that the U.S. government can do to address its lack of linguistic preparedness. For example, it can reevaluate its translation technology to intelligently separate diverse types of information. It also can and should identify all of the language resources that exist in the country, so that they cannot be hoarded by contractors.

Still, a more difficult task is to get the American society to see language not as something strange or un-American but rather as a valuable asset. To use a term more common in the capitalist parlance of this society, we need to see it as a competitive advantage. Government support for a new attitude toward language would encourage more people to become bilingual. We don't just mean the Anglos who are the typical targets of government funds for foreign language education but also the heritage speakers who remain at risk of losing their bilingualism. For these folks, such languages are not foreign but already familiar.

Down with Potatoes

In Iran, the phrase *Marg bar Amrika* (مرگ بر آمریکا) is often chanted at rallies and seen on signs held by unhappy protesters. The phrase is most commonly translated literally as "Death to America," but it actually means "Down with America." Hooman Majd, a former interpreter for Iranian President Ahmadinejad, has explained that "Death to America" is far too harsh of a translation. As Majd pointed out, Ahmadinejad also handed out potatoes in exchange for votes, after which protesters chanted *"Marg bar seeb zameeni!"* They were literally saying, "Death to potatoes," but it's pretty far-fetched to assume that their intention was to kill the spuds.[19]

Multilingual Intelligence

Imagine getting paid to read blogs and social media content all day long. Sound like a dream job? Well, there are people who do get paid to do it, but they don't exactly work from home in their pajamas, nor do they spend their days logged onto TMZ.com. You're much more likely to find them sitting in an office where a secret clearance is required because they work primarily for defense contractors. Those companies in turn work for the U.S. government, providing intelligence-gathering services.

They're translators—sort of. Their actual job titles can vary widely, depending on which company employs them, but their job almost always requires them to do translation. The difference is that they are paid not just to translate information but to analyze the content of what they are translating. Most commonly, they're known as media analysts, but don't let that seemingly simple title fool you. The job these bilingual individuals carry out is actually quite complex.[20]

Media analysts perform many functions, but their job boils down to one main thing: Find out what's going on in a given place and make sense of it. They track information from a country or region they know intimately—most often it's a place they grew up in or lived in extensively, and where they are likely to still have relatives and friends. They are highly specialized in the region and know it like the back of their hands.

And of course, they know the language, too. There has been extremely high demand in recent years for Chinese media analysts, as well as Arabic, Farsi, and Urdu, but also Russian, Serbian, Bulgarian, Ukrainian, and a host of other languages.

How do they do it exactly? Their work involves many different tasks. They find and track the sites of regional bloggers. They keep an eye on the local media environment and the different technologies being used. When critical communications "of ideological significance" are detected, they not only provide translations of this information but write up an analysis of what they think it really means for the local culture. They also identify key influencers and communicators in the media to create a media map of sociopolitical views. And they even measure the viral effectiveness of key messages and important themes. In addition, they use predictive analysis tools to identify trends and statements and their impact within a given region. Typically, even though they are expected to perform translation tasks, they do not have a professional background in translation but rather in journalism, media, or public relations.

In other words, they are expected to translate information not only at the level of "what does this say?" but at the level of "what does it mean?" and perhaps more important, when a critical situation arises, "what does it *really* mean?" While translators in most other fields are trained to come up with the best possible translation, in this particular setting, media analysts need to come up with many different ways to view a given situation as well as identify the strongest hypothesis for what the eventual outcome might be.

How is this information used for intelligence purposes? Consider this scenario. When Kim Jong-il's son Kim Jong-un was promoted to a senior position in the ruling Workers' Party, here's what U.S. intelligence wanted to know: Is the father grooming him to take over due to health issues? How is the public responding? Or take the example of uprisings in Syria. Intelligence gatherers asked these questions: What are the long-term prospects for President Bashar al-Assad's regime? According to local reports, is the country about to fall into civil war? Have chemical imports been rising, illicit or otherwise? How likely is the government to use its chemical weapons against its own people? These are the kinds of questions that media analysts deal with on an ongoing basis. They might not always be able to provide specific answers, but their job is to review the information they have in front of them and to provide the best possible summaries of likely scenarios. Their analysis may not always be what is considered "actionable intelligence," but it's intelligence nonetheless, and decisions are made based on their work each and every day.

Of Diplomats and Dialects

When you think of international diplomacy, chances are you think of heads of state and foreign ministers shaking hands, exchanging gifts, and discussing issues that matter to the countries they represent. But for all of those meetings to happen, a lot of work goes on behind the scenes. Just ask the U.S. Department of State (DOS), which maintains diplomatic relations between the United States and all sovereign countries, except Bhutan, Cuba, Iran, North Korea, and Taiwan. The DOS has eighteen thousand employees working in the Civil and Foreign Services alone. Logically, language plays a pretty important role in most foreign relations—and it has since 1781, when the Continental Congress hired its first translators.[21] Many of America's Founding Fathers, such as George Washington and Thomas Jefferson, relied on translators and interpreters.

For the document translation team at the State Department, there is never a dull moment. For example, whenever treaty negotiations take place, translators are there—either at the scene or behind the scenes—helping draft language that will be acceptable to both sides. They serve as linguistic experts, much in the same way attorneys from both sides serve as legal experts, to ensure that the terms mean exactly what they are meant to mean.

"It's an adrenaline rush," states Joseph Mazza, the department's translating division chief. "We joke that as a translator, you're all-powerful for fifteen minutes, because everyone is looking to you to make a decision. It's something you train for your entire career. All eyes are on you."[22] The nuances of a single word are debated. Drafts go back and forth. Discussions become heated and simmer down. And when a treaty is finally reached, all parties can breathe a sigh of relief. "It's a huge undertaking," observes Mazza, who manages a team of hundreds of freelance translators and a core staff of about twenty full-time in-house translators.

But treaties are just one of the many types of communications that the DOS translation team handles. Virtually any document that comes into the department in another language must be translated, including those in less common tongues. For example, Mazza recalls when President Obama received a letter from the king of Bhutan. The letter was written in Dzongkha, a language his team had never translated before due to the infrequency of official dealings with the country.

After searching high and low, Mazza and his team located a Dzongkha-language specialist. Unfortunately, after reviewing the text, the Dzongkha translator declined the job—for a surprising reason: The letter was evidently written not just in Dzongkha, but in Royal Dzongkha. "He told us that his eyes were not fit to read His Majesty's royal language," Mazza recalls. Eventually, the department located someone who found another translator, who was able to report that the letter contained greetings for a happy new year.

Of course, not all of the letters that come across the translation team's desk are so positive. "One of the jobs of my office is to screen all the mail that private citizens send to senior U.S. officials in other languages and summarize it wherever possible," Mazza explains. The letters span a wide range, from people professing their love to citizens writing in to request things like tractors, sometimes complete with photos. Sometimes, letters include threats to the president or the secretary of state. "When a threat comes in, it's an adrenaline rush of a different kind," he says. One of the more challenging parts of translating such letters is that they are often erratic and difficult to understand even in the source language. "It can be hard to follow the thread of what they are saying, but at the same time, you don't want to miss any clues that could be useful to investigators."

And then there are those important speeches, such as Obama's 2009 address to the international Muslim community, which was translated into more than two dozen languages. In addition to new languages, Mazza explains that with the Obama administration came a new focus on social media. His department began to translate streaming video captions into other languages, among many new projects. More than ever before, the nations of the world are engaging in one conversation.

Relationship Overload

In 2009, Secretary of State Hillary Clinton presented a goodwill gift to Foreign Minister Sergey Lavrov of Russia. The gift was a button that was meant to symbolize a "resetting" of the relationship between the two nations. However, instead of bearing the term "reset" (*perezagruzka*), the gift was labeled with the word *peregruzka*, which means "overloaded" or "overcharged." To make matters worse, the mistaken term was engraved in Latin characters rather than Cyrillic. Thankfully, the two diplomats ended up laughing at the mistranslation.[23]

Extreme Interpreting at the United Nations

The 132 interpreters at the United Nations transmit words that also have a major impact on international relations. They might not look like daredevils, but the work they do is certainly risky. "Our work is never short of exciting moments," explains Hossam Fahr, head of the interpreting service at the UN headquarters in New York.[24]

The pressure isn't just due to the type of content they interpret. Nor is it due to the fact that many of the people listening are influential diplomats and heads of state. It isn't even the rate of speech or the varied accents the interpreters have to be able to understand while simultaneously listening in one language and speaking in another. The real source of the stress for many UN interpreters is the fact that they are running a relay race because some interpreters have to wait until another finishes speaking before they can start interpreting into the other languages. "You're playing to virtuosos, so as you interpret, you're thinking of your colleagues who will be interpreting what you say into yet another language," Fahr points out. "If you stop, everybody stops."

What makes the work even more difficult is that, often, UN interpreters do not even get advance copies of the speeches they will be interpreting. Even when they do have them in advance, the speakers frequently deviate from what the prepared text says. "Often, we receive a copy of the speech after it's already been delivered," Fahr notes. "When you're already listening, comprehending, and speaking in another language at the same time, reading can actually be more of a hindrance than a help."

So how do the UN interpreters cope with such responsibility? "If you're addicted to adrenaline, you'll have no problem," Fahr says. "There is definitely such a thing as the interpreter's high, when you get an incredibly difficult statement and you render it well." And challenging speech abounds. Allegories, famous quotes, jokes, and proverbs fly at the interpreters, seemingly out of nowhere, and must be interpreted in real time. Sports metaphors, popular with American speakers, are especially tough for interpreters. "If a delegate says someone 'kicked off while we're at the fifty-yard line,' I think, 'Great, let me explain American football first, and then I can interpret that.'"

Not all interpreting work at the United Nations requires the same level of skill. For example, a meeting of the UN Security Council is more complex than a technical council meeting on migratory fish. For the latter, an interpreter can study terminology and come up to speed relatively quickly. Dealing with the drafting of a Security Council resolution takes a high degree of sensitivity and knowledge.

Fahr describes interpreting at the United Nations as a humbling experience. "The day I switch on the microphone and don't have those butterflies in my stomach and that feeling of edginess is the day I retire," he explains. "One good thing about our profession is that you cannot hide anything. Once you put an interpreter on the microphone, you know exactly who is who and what is what." And Fahr knows from personal experience what it's like to be unable to hide.

In 1992, Fahr was interpreting at the General Assembly as Boutros Boutros-Ghali was being sworn in as the secretary general of the United Nations. While interpreting, he made a mental note of the phrase *eminent statesman* in a speech designed to congratulate Boutros-Ghali on his new role as secretary general. Unfortunately, with the word *statesman* swirling around in his head, Fahr ended up saying that Boutros-Ghali was being sworn in as the secretary general of the United *States*. The General Assembly erupted in laughter.

As the president of the General Assembly explained that the interpreter had made a mistake, Fahr had to eat humble pie and interpret those words too. The irony of the situation was not lost on the crowd, who roared with laughter yet again and then broke out into applause. "As a result," Fahr says with a self-deprecating smirk, "I have the dubious distinction of being the only interpreter I know of to have received a round of applause in the General Assembly for messing up."

Interpreter in Chief

UN interpreters are not the only ones who have high-profile assignments. Take Harry Obst, who interpreted for seven U.S. presidents (Johnson, Nixon, Ford, Carter, Reagan, George H. W. Bush, and Clinton). In the process, he has helped secure congenial foreign relations for the U.S. government over a period of three decades.[25]

Not only did Obst interpret, but he frequently found himself taking on responsibilities that extended far beyond his job description.[26] For example, during one meeting between U.S. President Lyndon B. Johnson and German Chancellor Kurt Kiesinger, Kiesinger posed a complicated question about NATO missile defenses. Johnson hesitated for a moment, stumped. Seizing on the hesitation, the German chancellor went for a long-deferred bathroom break.

As soon as Johnson and Obst found themselves alone in the room, the president turned to Obst, and asked in his heavy Texan drawl: "Mr. Interpreter, how shall we answer that?" Johnson knew that Obst had been briefed extensively on the necessary facts and figures. Obst quickly supplied the necessary information to the president. When the German leader returned, Johnson impressed him with a well-informed answer, after which the chancellor complimented him for a military expertise that Johnson was not otherwise known for.

Another time when a difficult question came up, this time during a White House meeting, Johnson announced, "Let me consult the interpreter." To his consternated advisers, the president explained, "They've been around." Johnson sometimes asked advice from veteran interpreters, realizing that they had worked under previous administrations, giving them personal knowledge of foreign leaders and their negotiating styles.

Later, when Carter was in office, the president's chief speech writer called Obst with a request from the president for his keynote speech in July 1978 at the Airlift Memorial in Berlin. Carter wanted Obst to craft a sentence in German, similar to Kennedy's famous line "*Ich bin ein Berliner!*" Obst, wanting to avoid German umlauts and other sounds that might be difficult to pronounce, came up with "*Was immer sei, Berlin bleibt frei*" (No matter what, Berlin will remain free). White House aides considered this sentence "too corny and not presidential," but Carter liked it and put it at the end of his speech. The morning after the speech, Obst's linguistic concoction was the headline in all major Berlin newspapers and in most other German dailies.

Carter also experienced the opposite end of the spectrum when it came to interpreters and media coverage. One unfortunate experience made *Time* magazine's list of Top 10 Most Embarrassing Moments.[27] In late December 1977, Carter touched down in Warsaw,

Poland. Because the State Department had no staff interpreter for Polish, they had hired Steven Seymour, a freelance Russian–English interpreter who was Polish by birth and had gone to college in Poland. Though Seymour was not a Polish interpreter by trade, he was asked to interpret anyway. Unfortunately, he received the president's prepared speech only a minute or two ahead of time, instead of hours in advance, which would have allowed him time to fully prepare.

Due to the frosty relations between the Polish and the U.S. governments at the time, the U.S. delegation had to wait outside for the presidential plane in the equally freezing rain for three hours.

Hindered by all these factors, Seymour went on to render such innocent statements by President Carter as "when I left the United States" into Polish as "when I abandoned the United States." He also accidentally interpreted "your desires for the future" as "your lusts for the future," a sexually laden and particularly uncharacteris-

The Kennedy Mistranslation Myth

In 1963, U.S. President John F. Kennedy gave a speech after the Berlin Wall was erected to express solidarity with the citizens of Berlin. His few words of German—"*Ich bin ein Berliner*," which means "I am a Berliner"—made an immediate impact on his audience. But rumors soon began to spread that Kennedy had botched the grammar and mistakenly called himself a jelly donut also known as a Berliner. In fact, his sentence was grammatically correct, and his German-speaking listeners knew that he was not referring to the pastry. Robert Lochner, who helped Kennedy write the speech, was a chief

German interpreter during World War II. Kennedy had also practiced the speech in front of many Germans, including Willy Brandt, the mayor of Berlin. In this case, there was no mistranslation.[28]

tic expression for a president who was known for his deeply held religious convictions. The Polish press had a field day with the comments, and once the U.S. media got wind of it, so did they. (President Carter took the incident in stride, and Seymour went on to have a distinguished career as a translator—in Russian, not Polish.)

506 Language Pairs for the Price of a Cup of Coffee

As the writer Umberto Eco observed, "The language of Europe is translation." Indeed, there are quite a few languages spoken by the 736 members of the European Parliament who serve the European Union (EU). How do they communicate? Through interpreters, of course. The EU is the largest transnational democratic electorate in the world, and it handles a mind-boggling number of languages and assignments. The twenty-three languages spoken by the members of the parliament are Bulgarian, Czech, Danish, Dutch, English, Estonian, Finnish, French, German, Greek, Hungarian, Irish, Italian, Latvian, Lithuanian, Maltese, Polish, Portuguese, Romanian, Slovak, Slovene, Spanish, and Swedish.

While twenty-three languages might not sound like much, when you consider all of the potential combinations (Swedish into Greek,

Danish into Estonian, French into Maltese, and so on), this means that interpreting services must be provided in 506 different language combinations. In addition, they also provide interpreters for nonofficial languages when needed, such as Arabic, Russian, Chinese, Farsi, and Turkish.

Interpreting for the European Parliament is challenging not just because of the words that must be converted from one language into another but because the interpreters have to pay attention to things like context, innuendo, and body language. Not only that, but sometimes the content can be difficult to interpret or even embarrassing. After all, political debates can get extremely heated. At a meeting of the European Parliament in 2003, Silvio Berlusconi compared Martin Schultz, a German member of the Parliament, to a Nazi. "I know that in Italy there is a man producing a film on Nazi concentration camps," Berlusconi said. "I shall put you forward for the role of *kapo*—you would be perfect." (The term *kapo* refers to a prisoner in a Nazi concentration camp who was assigned by the SS guards to supervise forced labor or carry out administrative tasks in the camp.) Just imagine the reaction of the interpreter who had to convey these offensive words in German to Schultz.

How many people does it take to make all this interpreting happen? The European Parliament has twenty-two linguistic units, 344 staff interpreters, and 150 support staff. At a single plenary session in Strasbourg in 2011, there were more than a thousand interpreters on hand. (Not all of them were full-time staff interpreters. Some were brought in just for the event.) In total, the interpreters for the European Parliament delivered 87,400 interpretation days in 2009 and 109,667 in 2010.[29]

Olga Cosmidou, who oversees the Directorate-General for Interpretation and Conferences, is at the helm of these activities. The interpreting is impressive in terms of both volume and impact. Many members of the parliament simply cannot communicate without interpreters.

Yet even though interpreters are essential for the parliament to actually do its work, people are sometimes quick to complain about the costs. Olga shrugs off the criticism. "It's the cost of democracy," she says. How much does it cost exactly? About €2.3 per citizen per year, or less than an average cup of coffee. If you ask us, that's pretty good value for money.

Broadcasting Global Politics

When laws are debated by elected representatives and leaders are elected throughout the world, we rely largely on foreign correspondents to bring us the news and put it into the proper context.

Rob Gifford, who began learning Mandarin Chinese in the UK and later in China, is one of these journalists. You might recognize Rob's name from his many radio reports during his seven years as the China correspondent for NPR; you may have read *China Road*, Rob's book about a trip from the east coast to the far west in China; or perhaps you've read his articles in the *Economist*, for which he presently works as the China editor.[30]

After more than twenty years of working in China for some of the most prestigious international news organizations, Rob speaks fluent Chinese and follows China closely. Yet, even he relies on professional translation and interpretation when it comes to specialized topics.

For instance, in 2005 Rob conducted an interview with then-minister of commerce, Bo Xilai. Though Rob approached the interview with the self-assurance of a Chinese expert, he quickly realized that he had overstepped his limits. In fact, his language repertoire simply did not include Minister Bo's high-level economic talk on trade wars and technical vocabulary on currency evaluations. As Bo responded (in Chinese) to each new question with, "As I just explained . . ." it became painfully clear that both sides had recognized the problem. Fortunately, Rob had recorded the interview, so he could have his assistant review and translate it again to ensure accurate reporting.

The nature of late-breaking news does not always make it easy for journalists to get professional interpreters as quickly as they need them. Rob recalls traveling through an area of Gansu in northern China that was formerly part of Tibet and is still widely inhabited by Tibetans. Seeing a group of young monks in an Internet café and wanting to interview them about their situation and their view on Tibet, he asked whether any of them spoke Mandarin. After some giggling they all pointed out one young man, obviously better educated than the others, given that he had learned Chinese. But as Rob explains, he faced a grave difficulty: Because of a lack of a Tibetan interpreter, a single educated Tibetan monk would now be representing not only the opinion of his friends in the café but also potentially "what eight million Tibetans think." The point? Even the best-prepared journalist cannot always function without a professional interpreter or translator.[31]

CHAPTER 3

Doing Business and Crossing Borders in Translation

People won't buy what they can't understand.

—Donald A. DePalma,
American author and global business adviser

The Minimalists: Starbucks and Apple

Companies work hard to create brands that are recognizable throughout the world. For many, the quest for international recognition can even extend beyond just their products and into their corporate logo. Take Starbucks, for instance. For the company's fortieth anniversary in 2011, it removed all traces of text from its logo. Namely, it got rid of the words *Starbucks Coffee*. (The current logo is actually the fourth version. The first logo was created in the 1970s and included the words *Starbucks Coffee, Tea, and Spice*.) Creating a wordless logo for a brand that was already well-known made it easier for Starbucks to move into other countries—especially the ones whose languages do not rely on Latin characters.

How do global brands in other sectors handle this issue? One of the best examples comes from outside the food and beverage industry, in spite of its name. Apple, known all over the world for its simplicity of design and advertising, has managed to come up with creative advertising campaigns that require only the bare minimum of translation work. When the iPod Shuffle came out, the company launched a campaign based around just two words. The marketing initiative featured the tiny mp3 player held between two fingers and flanked by the words *small talk*. Just two basic words. Easy to translate, right?

Actually, those two seemingly innocent words present plenty of translation challenges. Think about it. If you had to describe the phrase *small talk* to someone who did not understand it, what words would you use? Chances are, you would discuss the importance of exchanging pleasantries. You might describe asking someone about the weather. Basically, you'd be describing something superficial, and perhaps unimportant. How would that translate exactly, and would your explanation of the concept reflect well on Apple?

Obviously, many languages don't use the words *small* and *talk* in the same way that English does. The phrase, while catchy in English, needed to be adapted significantly for most other markets. In fact, to have the most impact, it had to be adapted differently even for countries that speak the same language. So in Latin American Spanish, the message Apple used was not *small talk*, but rather *mira quién habla*, which means "look who's talking." In Spanish for Spain, the phrase was *ya sabe hablar*, which has a double meaning— it's the phrase a proud parent would use to say that their child "is already talking" or more literally, "already knows how to talk." In France, the phrase used was *donnez-lui de la voix*, which means something like "let him speak." However, head to French Canada, and the message was *petit parleur, grand faiseur*, which means "says little, does much."

Minimizing the text in your branding and marketing can be an effective technique, but it does not necessarily make translation easy or simple. In cases like Apple's, an entire atmosphere of content must be translated to support those customers who speak other languages and want to know how to use their products. Just think of all the online help information that must be translated—not to mention the product literature that ships with any Apple product. Starbucks isn't exempt from translation either, in spite of having a product that requires little explanation and a brand with no words. The words *Starbucks Coffee* might no longer appear on the coffee cup itself, but visit the company's website, and you'll see that this phrase appears on each of its international web properties, most of which have an array of translated content.

When Mistranslations Cost Millions

Banking and financial services giant HSBC had a popular *Assume Nothing* campaign, but the phrase was mistranslated as "Do Nothing" in several countries. How to repair the damage done to the brand? A $10 million rebranding initiative soon followed.[1]

IKEA's Danish Doormats

It's easy to see why IKEA is so popular all over the world. The Scandinavian retailer is known for its streamlined self-assembly furniture with modern designs at affordable prices. The company's simple style even extends into its branding and marketing, for which it relies very little on text. Compared to many retailers, the company employs just the bare minimum of text to tout its wares, relying more on images.

IKEA depends heavily on catalog sales and invests significantly in this printed medium, which consumes a reported 70 percent of its annual marketing budget. In 2011, the company published nearly two hundred million catalogs in sixty-one editions and twenty-nine different languages.[2] Mirroring its catalog, the company also favors image-based description on its forty country-specific websites. IKEA offers more than twelve thousand products, and translates its packaging and labeling into as many as thirty languages, depending on the product in question. For a market like North America, labels are typically translated into English, French, and Spanish. (Of course, even IKEA has a blooper of a product name from time to time, such as the Fartfull and Jerker computer desks, which the company sold in 2005, much to the amusement of English speakers.)

In light of the importance of its catalog sales, the company's light-handed approach to words can be a tremendous advantage when it comes to translation. Most of IKEA's instructions are pictorial in nature—you'll rarely see any words on them, providing a rather universal appeal.

The few words that IKEA does use in its marketing—its product names—hold a unique appeal for its customers. Most of its items are named after places in the Nordic region, so for many of its customers, the product names have an exotic, cool, and quirky feel. People from many countries might even venture to say that some of the terms sound downright charming. Unless you're from Denmark, that is.

No one likes to see their country called a doormat. But that's what the Danes often deal with whenever they walk into an IKEA store. Many of its cheaper products, including rugs, mats, and other floor coverings, such as Bellinge, Helsingör, Köge, Nivå, Roskilde, Sindal, and Strib, are named after places in Denmark. So, it's understandable that even the Danes, who are ranked by some sources as the happiest people on earth, would not be thrilled to have their country associated with places where people wipe their feet.

Two Danish academics, Klaus Kjöller of the University of Copenhagen and Tröls Mylenberg of the University of Southern Denmark, conducted a detailed analysis of product names used in the IKEA catalog. The findings of their research showed that Swedish names were used for the higher-end products, such as upholstered furniture, bookcases, and storage for flat screen televisions and multimedia devices. Norwegian towns were used for bedroom furniture, while Finnish place names made it into the dining room.[3]

The researchers found that IKEA's naming convention portrayed Denmark as inferior to Sweden. The historic rivalry between the two countries would seem to lend some credence to this argument. Sweden has often emerged victorious over Denmark. In fact, Norway once belonged to the Danes until the Swedes took it away from them. But is IKEA really gloating to Denmark through its product names? Let's put it this way, IKEA didn't drop the Danish-named products. In fact, it continues to sell a toilet seat, Öresund, which is named after a strait of water that separates Sweden from Denmark. Coincidence?

While IKEA has been forthcoming about the fact that it names these items after Denmark, the accusation that it is purposely dissing the Danes has been met with, well, disdain. Officials from IKEA claim that the product names have been around for decades, and that the employee who came up with the place names retired long ago. They have also refused to change the names, arguing that their naming system simplifies the experience for the customer.

Many Danes say that, even if the names were created on purpose to poke fun, they don't really mind, chalking it up to the well-known competitive spirit between the Nordic countries. As proof that they're not that bothered, the Danish population has continued to buy the products—yes, even those with names of their homeland that they often find underfoot.

Hog Wild for Harley

He sits, hands on the throttle, ready to ride. Faded black leather covers his clunky boots and is zipped up around his torso. He revs the motorcycle's engine, with its trademark thundering sound. He is grateful for the customizations he made to the exhaust system to amplify the bike's roar. He's fifty-two years old, and he loves his Harley, an iconic symbol of the American lifestyle. Yet he doesn't live in California, Nevada, or Arizona. And his name isn't John, Mike, or Bubba. He's not from around these parts. He has lived in Japan his entire life, and his name is Yamada Tarō.

Japan is full of Yamada Tarōs—it's a stereotypical Japanese name, the equivalent of John Smith in English. Even though the country has many homegrown brands like Honda, Suzuki, Kawasaki, and Yamaha, Harley-Davidson is the local market leader when it comes to motorbikes. The Japanese didn't become Harley fans by some stroke of luck. Translation helped make it happen. Founded in 1903, the company has been translating its product information into other languages for nearly as long as it has been in business. If a Harley-Davidson enthusiast in Japan wants to learn how to operate his bike or how to customize it, he'll turn to his owner manual. And it had better be in Japanese. Harley's biggest international market outside the United States is Japan, and it has been for a number of years.[4]

Translators who work on technical manuals often joke that no one ever reads the fruits of their labor. Not so in the case of Harley-Davidson customers, who frequently devour the owner manuals to learn how to make adjustments to their bikes. Today, the company translates into twenty languages, such as Czech, Greek, Norwegian, and Turkish. Some brand-specific terms present special challenges, such as *jiffy stand*, which means "kick stand," or *derby cover*, which is the cover for the clutch, so named because of its resemblance to a derby hat at one point in the brand's history.

Translation is certainly a critical enabler of Harley-Davidson's global revenue. Today, its international business accounts for more than 30 percent of total revenue. However, sometimes the barriers to business go beyond just culture and language. Take the case of China, where motorcycling is not widely recognized as a recreational activity but rather as a means of affordable transportation. There are also significant legal barriers to overcome. Due to the popularity of small scooters in China, many large urban areas have placed restrictions on all two-wheeled vehicles to reduce noise and environmental pollution.[5]

While China remains a tough nut to crack for the Milwaukee-based motorbike manufacturer, the company enjoys success in many other nations. Not what you might expect for a brand that most people associate with being quintessentially American.

Baby, You Can Drive My Car

Auto manufacturers have often seen that a car model name that works well in one country must be modified to have success in another. Ford launched a car in Europe named Kuga, which means "plague" in Croatian and Serbian. Mitsubishi produced an off-road vehicle called the Pajero, an offensive term for "wanker" in some Spanish-speaking countries. The Honda Fitta had to be renamed to the Honda Jazz for the Nordic market because *fitta* is a profane word for female genitals. One car that didn't have to be renamed? The Chevy Nova. Contrary to popular belief, the word *nova* is not easily confused with the words *no va* (doesn't go) in Spanish because they are pronounced differently, with stress on different syllables. General Motors reported that the Nova actually surpassed its expectations for sales in markets like Venezuela.

The *Economist* Speaks Chinese

Of course, some imports have experienced the exact opposite of Harley-Davidson in China—wild popularity without really having to try. This is the case with the *Economist*. The weekly magazine has a team of such devoted fans that they routinely volunteer their free time to translate the popular British periodical into Chinese. That's three hundred pages' worth of articles per week.[6]

They're called the Eco Team, a group of volunteers connected through a web-based interface. Every two weeks, they produce and publish a Chinese-language version of two full magazines, making them available online at no charge. Founded in 2006, the forum was originally funded through donations. An insurance broker, Shi Yi, heads up the effort.[7] More than two hundred volunteer translators form the full group, and it takes about forty members to produce each issue.

The process the team uses is straightforward. First, translation volunteers pick stories to translate based on their areas of interest. Another volunteer oversees the process, moderates the group, tracks the assigned articles, and monitors their completion status. Once an article is translated, other members of the community use a comment section to suggest improvements to the translations. Last, an editor applies the corrections and delivers the final proofed version for publication. Their volunteer translation task is not a simple one. The *Economist* is notorious for its wordplay and double meanings, requiring a high level of proficiency in English. Consider this actual sentence from an article in the February 4, 2012, print edition: "Insiders crow that the gumshoes found no smoking gun." Try replacing the key terms in that sentence with synonyms—in English—and you'll get a sense of the translators' challenge.

These translating fans are not paid for their work, and they do not charge for the end product. In fact, they encourage the individuals who visit their website to subscribe to the *Economist* in English. It's a noncommercial effort that is focused on sharing knowledge, and because they are not making any money from it and actually drive new subscribers to the *Economist*, they don't believe themselves to be in violation of any copyright.

So far, the publishers of the *Economist* seem to agree. As Andrew Baio reported in the *New York Times*, Mr. Yi met with the publication's editorial staff, including executive editor John Micklethwait. Yi's team was granted approval to continue their pro bono translation work for the time being.[8] It's no wonder why. In May 2011, one of the site's moderators mentioned that it had surpassed ninety thousand registered users. At no cost and minimal risk to the publisher, it's not a bad way for a magazine to open up a new market, especially considering the changing nature of traditional publishing. (The *Economist* isn't the only publisher benefiting from this trend. Recently, Chinese mothers have formed online groups at websites such as Dreamkidland.cn, where English-speaking mothers can translate children's books into Chinese for their children. Many of the translations have been used by publishers to produce actual books. And because the mothers ask for input from the children, kids actually have a say in which books get translated.)

The volunteers do put themselves at risk, however. Because some of the magazine's articles cover taboo subjects, such as Tibet, the team performs the translations within the safety of a protected forum. The Eco Team also advises its members to err on the side of caution and avoid controversial topics to protect the project itself and make sure that it is allowed to continue. Still, for these fans, the risk seems worth the reward. Not only do thousands of Chinese readers get access to the *Economist* thanks to the fruits of the team's labor, but in the process of translating, the volunteers become exposed to news from around the world and the associated social, political, and economic concepts embedded in the articles. Is China warming to the West through translation? Perhaps.

Translation Error Leads to Panic on the Trading Floor

Guan Xiangdong, a reporter for the China News Service, wrote a story in 2009 about the impact of a possible appreciation of Chinese currency. A bad translation of her report ended up causing chaos in the world's foreign exchange market, leading the U.S. dollar to take a major tumble as traders and fund managers began dropping dollars in favor of Asian currencies. The erroneous text was corrected, but the damage had already been done.

Money Talks—in Many Languages

Most translation is not done on a volunteer basis. It's performed by professionals who are paid to do this work. In fact, it may just be the biggest industry that most people have never heard of. As of 2012, the market for language services was worth more than $33 billion. Just fifty of the top-earning firms account for nearly $4 billion in revenue. More than twenty-six thousand companies throughout the world sell translation and interpreting services.[9]

Even during the global economic downturn, while performance in most sectors slumped, language service providers (LSPs) kept on growing. In fact, the language services market grew each year during the recession. The majority of these firms are small and medium-size family-owned businesses, often founded by translators. Many of them are also minority owned and women owned. But don't be fooled—just because they are small does not mean they are not attractive to investors. It is common for these companies to grow each year at rates that exceed 20 percent, even during times of recession. And profit margins frequently exceed 30 percent.

Why are these businesses so successful, even during a downturn? The answer is simple—translation makes it possible for companies to increase their revenue. There isn't a business operating in more than one country that doesn't rely on translation, at least at some level, to increase its sales. Companies in nearly every industry spend money on translation, but those businesses part with their precious dollars, yen, and euros only because they believe it can help them generate more of them. And they are absolutely right.

One study from industry research firm Common Sense Advisory found, based on a survey of 2,430 consumers in eight countries, that 72.4 percent of consumers were more likely to buy a product if provided with information in their own language. In fact, more than half of the respondents (56.2 percent) said that the ability to obtain information in their own language was even *more important to them than price*.[10] Yes, you read that right. If you're trying to stop prices from eroding in your industry, language can be a differentiator.

Research from the European Commission reveals similar findings. A 2011 study was based on a Gallup survey of language preferences among Internet users in twenty-three European countries. The study found that, when given a choice of languages, nine out of ten Internet users *always visited websites in their native languages*. One in five Europeans said they never browse in other languages, and 42 percent claimed that they never purchase products and services in other languages.[11] And keep in mind, that's in Europe, where multilingualism is fairly common. What this means is that even when people are proficient in other languages, they still prefer to buy in their native languages.

The bottom line is this: Translation has and always will be important for any company that wants to do business in multiple markets. If customers are going to buy the products and services a company sells, they expect to receive information in their native languages. It's not about being politically or linguistically correct.

In an age of global competition and increased access to information, translating content into other languages is about being business savvy.

Inserito Scidulam

So far we've been discussing the importance of translation for global business, but let's not forget that most business transactions take place at the local level. In most parts of the world, all you have to do is walk up to an automatic teller machine (ATM) to see how translation contributes to these local economies. The estimated two million ATMs worldwide enable customers to take out money, make deposits, and conduct business conveniently on their own instead of going into a branch where they would need to rely on humans.

Get off a plane in Barcelona, and you'll find ATMs in Basque, Catalan, and Spanish for the locals, plus English and French for the tourists. Make a withdrawal in Ireland, and you'll see not only English and Irish Gaelic for the natives, but Polish for the sizable immigrant community. If you're in Bolivia, you can take out money in Aymara, Spanish, or Quechua (the language once used by the Incas). Step up to make a deposit in New Zealand, and you'll see options in English and Māori, as well as Chinese, French, German, Japanese, and Korean. Go to South Africa, and you can manage your bank accounts in Afrikaans, English, Sepedi, Venda, Xhosa, and Zulu. Visit the Vatican, and you'll even find an ATM with the Latin words *Inserito scidulam quaeso ut faciundam cognoscas rationem* (Please insert your ATM card and enter your PIN) on the touch screen.

With few exceptions, no matter where you go in the world, you'll find multiple languages on the touch screens and buttons of these cash dispensers. Multilingualism is a natural state for nearly every society in the world, but when it comes to ATMs, providing language access contributes to a healthy economy. For tourists to spend money in your community, giving them an easy way to obtain that money is a no-brainer. But this isn't just important for tourists. The refugees and immigrants who live in your community can deposit their checks, pay their bills, and contribute to local commerce more easily when they can do so in their native languages.

The crass truth is that businesses ultimately care far more about the money in a wallet than they do about the language of the person who has the power to open it. Translation simply makes it easier for people to hand over their cash. Most companies will translate information only if it makes business sense. That—not political correctness—is the main reason you'll find ATMs displaying Hmong in Wisconsin, Vietnamese in California, and Inuktitut in Canada. Translation is good for business—not just on a global scale, but at the microeconomic level of your local city block.

The Most Translated Airline in the World

Many travel-sector companies rely on translation to increase revenue, and United Airlines is no exception. United is the world's leading airline, with nearly eighty-seven thousand employees and more than seven hundred planes. It operates in 170 countries around the world, and is one of the few airlines that flies to all six inhabited continents. So, as you might have guessed, it relies on translation to serve its customers in the many languages they speak.

In most parts of the world, gone are the days of driving to a travel agency and printing out paper tickets. These days, it's all about the web. Booking flights online reduces costs and wait time. So, understandably, United makes its website available in multiple languages—exactly eleven of them, in fact, with plans to add more in the future.

"Each month, we translate between one hundred forty-four thousand and three hundred fifty-five thousand words into eleven languages," explains Theophannie Theodore, senior manager of international reliability—eCommerce at United.[12] However, she points out that not all of the words are new. Like most savvy companies with experience in translation, rather than translate every single piece of content from scratch, the company uses translation software to identify previously translated phrases and sentences. (We'll discuss this technology further in Chapter Seven.)

The types of content that United translates cover a broad range of subjects, from informational pages on its website to full-fledged applications that allow passengers to create a new booking, set up a frequent-flyer account, or update a profile. "We even translate signs for the airport and check-in kiosks," Theodore points out.

Terminology in the airline industry can be especially tricky— just consider terms like *record locator*, *red-eye*, and *in-flight entertainment*, which do not have direct translations in many languages. For this reason, each time United launches a new language, they develop a glossary of airline-specific nomenclature and terminology related to the travel industry. Terminology can pose additional challenges when airlines merge, as they often do these days.

But is all of this tedious language work really worth the trouble? Yes, especially in an increasingly global economy. Theodore cites a clear example: For many years, the China site had only a basic amount of content translated into Chinese. If a customer tried to book a ticket, nearly all of the remaining content was in English. In

April 2010, the company launched a translated version of the booking engine in Chinese. "Within just months after the launch, we saw ticketed online revenue increase by 300 percent year over year," Theophannie points out.

It isn't so difficult to understand why translation matters in an industry that takes people from one country to another. But United links the importance of translation to an even broader vision. "Translation is important in any industry that has a global e-commerce presence," remarks Theodore. "Just think of it this way: Would you make a purchase on a site in a language that you don't understand?" Most of the world would answer with a resounding no.

Fly in the Ultimate Comfort

In 1977, Braniff International Airways put out an advertisement to promote the leather seats they'd installed in their new first-class cabins. However, the campaign's slogan, "Fly in leather," was translated for Spanish-speaking markets as *Vuela en cuero*. In Spanish, this was equivalent to saying, "Fly naked," implying a more comfortable flight for some travelers, not to mention a much easier job for airport security screeners.

Ice(landic), Ice(landic), Baby

When you think of Iceland, what comes to mind? Perhaps you think of Björk or Sigur Rós, some of the country's musicians who have risen to international fame. Or maybe you call up a mental image of some of its famous glaciers, geysers, and volcanoes, such as Eyjafjallajökull, whose pronunciation stumped news commentators around the world after its infamous eruption in April 2010, which caused nearly a week of delays in air travel across western and northern Europe. Iceland is considered by many travelers to be an exotic and mystical destination. But its language is perhaps even more mysterious and elusive.

Perhaps that's why it's so interesting that Icelandair puts the Icelandic language front and center on all of its flights. Rather than shying away from its native language, which many people find daunting, the airline dares its passengers to give the difficult tongue a try. It isn't just the fact that the flight attendants make announcements in Icelandic; hearing the language of a local air carrier is something you expect no matter where you travel in the world. No, Icelandair takes its language presence to a new level entirely, integrating it into the complete experience.

As you board the plane, you'll notice a translation on every single seat. The company uses the headrests to teach passengers how to say basic phrases like *thank you* and *good night* in Icelandic. Get to your seat, and you're greeted by yet another translation, which is stamped on your pillow. It's an Icelandic lullaby, written in Icelandic, with the translation next to it in English:

> *Bye, bye and hushabye*
> *Can you see the swans fly?*
> *Now half asleep in bed I lie*
> *Awake with half an eye*
> *Heyho and welladay*
> *Over hills and far away*
> *That's where the little children stray*
> *To find the lambs at play.*

Bí, bí og blaka
álftirnar kvaka.
Ég læt sem ég sofi
en samt mun ég vaka.
Bíum, bíum, bamba,
börnin litlu ramba
fram á fjallakamba
ad leita sér lamba.

After you sit down, check out the in-flight entertainment, which features a language-learning program for Icelandic. Plug in your headphones, and you'll hear Icelandic music. Turn on the television, and you'll see an entire category of movies in Icelandic (with English subtitles, of course).

Open up the airline's magazine, and you'll see a letter from the CEO in which he talks with pride about the Icelandic language. Order a children's meal, and you'll see an Icelandic story on the lid, written in Icelandic and accompanied by an English translation. Even the airline's coffee cup promotes Icelandic phrases. In other words, Icelandair does not miss a chance to showcase its language in front of the 1.5 million passengers it transports each year.

"Iceland and Icelandic are what Icelandair is founded on," says Guðmundur Óskarsson, director of marketing and business development at Icelandair. "Everything from our route network to the way we address our customers in written or spoken language has a strong connection to Icelandic culture and heritage." He goes on to explain, "The Icelandic language is one of the tools we use to differentiate ourselves from the competition."[13]

Why is promoting the Icelandic language so important? There are many reasons. It's one of the oldest living languages in Europe, dating back to the Viking times. Rather than adopt words from other languages, Icelandic has a policy of reappropriating old words and giving them new meanings. For example, the term *rafmagn* (electricity) means "amber power." The word *sími* (telephone) originally meant "cord." Icelandic has only about three hundred thousand speakers, so ensuring its survival is important. Iceland even devotes a special day to the language, Dagur Íslenskrar Tungu (Icelandic Language Day), each year on November 16. But most important, encapsulated within the Icelandic language is a unique way of viewing the world. Most airlines use translation to reach customers in other parts of the world. Icelandair uses translation to bring its world to the customer.

Houston, We Need an Interpreter

Translation is also important for people who wish to travel beyond the realm of Earth. Huh? Yes, translation even happens in outer space. We're not talking about science fiction, though translation has certainly made a splash there, too. We're talking about interpreting for the International Space Station (ISS).

For many of us, a trip into space is the stuff of fantasies. Not for Irina Yashkova, a graduate of the prestigious Monterey Institute of International Studies. In the fourteen years she has worked for the ISS, she has interpreted for thirty expeditions into space, and more than fifty space walks. When someone says, "Houston, we have a problem," it might just be Yashkova's voice that interprets that message.[14]

Yashkova is a member of an elite team of highly trained interpreters who are certified flight controllers and work around the clock supporting real-time operations in orbit. Mission control centers in Houston, Tsukuba, Huntsville, Munich, and Moscow regularly communicate with each other to coordinate activities on the ground and in space. When Russian crew members speak in Russian to each other, the remaining mission control centers listen in on the conversations, which are simultaneously interpreted into English by Yashkova or one of her colleagues.

Yashkova's job description might strike many people as unusual, but her daily work is quite regimented. Each morning, she interprets for teleconference and videoconference calls, enabling specialists in Russia and the United States to communicate. The people who require her services may include engineers, medical professionals, trainers, designers, and managers. In the afternoon, she typically interprets for face-to-face meetings between individuals involved in the ISS from the sixteen different countries participating. Often, the primary language used for meetings is English, so she interprets into Russian and transfers the Russian-speaking participants' comments and questions back into English.

In spite of having access to interpreters, international crew members are actually required to have a certain level of proficiency in both Russian and English before they are allowed to go into space. They must have a basic proficiency in both languages because they will need to communicate with ground staff in either language. Those who do not already speak Russian must participate in an immersion program in Russian for six weeks. They live with a family, take intensive courses, and participate in cultural events. Those who do not speak English must come up to speed very quickly by taking classes too.

But during the space walks, interpreters are on standby in case of any emergencies. When tricky situations take place, all eyes are on the interpreter. "Essentially, the life of the crew member is in your hands," Yashkova notes. Also at risk and in her hands? A very expensive space station.

Even before they can go up into space, the crew members rely a great deal on interpreters to complete their ground training. In Yashkova's case, before interpreting for Expedition 6 space walks, she had to go through the entire space walk training along with three astronauts (two American, one Russian) for a period of nine months. "Space walks are very complex," she points out. "There are hundreds of connectors and very complex tasks that the crew members carry out while in orbit." Because of the complexity, the role of language is extremely important. "Mission-critical procedures used by the crew members have to be translated," Yashkova explains.

As an interpreter, Yashkova rarely does written translation work—most of that is handled by a small team of translators who specialize in the written translation side, ensuring that all of the terminology complies with industry standards. However, she, along with the team of translators, is heavily involved in terminology and glossary development. "Our operational nomenclature has thousands of entries for life-support systems, food items, and so on," Yashkova explains. "Interpreters have to be familiar with each and every term." She points out that interpreters use the operational glossaries as training tools only. When they are in the midst of interpreting, they have to rely on their own memories.

Could the space program actually function without translation? "I think it would be very difficult, almost impossible," Yashkova points out. "Many flight controllers, engineers, doctors, and ground specialists speak English or Russian on a basic conversational level.

Using professional interpretation enables them to concentrate fully on engineering, management, and safety tasks, so their ideas can be rendered into another language accurately and precisely." She adds, "When professional interpreters create an illusion that international specialists speak 'the same language,' that is when our job is well done."

Naming the Newest Space Travelers

Astronauts, cosmonauts, and taikonauts all carry out the same essential duties—they just do them for different space agencies and nations. The terms *astronaut* and *cosmonaut* (from Russian космонавт) have been around at least since the launch of their countries' space travel ambitions in the 1950s. Both terms simply mean "space sailors" or "space navigators." However, in recent years, when China began its own extraterrestrial explorations, Western journalists were quick to embrace a new term to refer to the Chinese astronauts. The term they latched on to was *taikonaut*, a hybrid of the Chinese word for outer space, *tai kong* or 太空 (literally, "great emptiness") and the English word *astronaut*. The closest term linguistically to *taikonaut* in Chinese is *tai kong ren* or 太空人, but the term never caught on in China—it's used only in Hong Kong and Taiwan and was first introduced by a Malaysian journalist. In China, the term *hangtianyuan or* 航天员 (sky sailor) is the preferred name for space travelers. An older but related term that predated the Chinese space program was *yuhangyuan* or 宇航员 (space sailor). And which word does the Chinese government use for its official publications in English? Not taikonaut, but rather, astronaut.[15]

Flowery Words

Back on planet Earth, we arrive at the Bellagio. From the opulent Chihuly glass ceiling in its lobby to the sumptuous fabrics in its guest rooms, the upscale Las Vegas hotel exudes elegance and luxury. The hotel prides itself on meticulous service and exceeding guest expectations. One in every four guests at the Bellagio comes from another country, predominantly Brazil, Mexico, Japan, Germany, France, Portugal, Italy, and Spain. For its most elite guests, the Bellagio goes even further to cater to every whim. It isn't uncommon for the hotel staff to run last-minute errands and to source hard-to-find items for these top-tier visitors.

Once, when a well-heeled guest at the hotel decided that she would like to have an orchid in her suite, she didn't think twice about asking a Bellagio staff member to go and fetch one on her behalf. Even though it was around 11 p.m. when Erden Kendigelen saw the request come in, he did not bat an eyelash. His job was to take care of exactly these types of needs for his customers. Kendigelen had his marching orders.

He quickly ran off to one of the hotel's gift shops to obtain the orchids, placing them in a gift bag and tying it with a beautiful ribbon. He then proceeded to hand-deliver them to her suite. When the guest answered the door, she was happy to see that her request had been fulfilled so expediently, but was surprised that the staff member had put them in a bag. When she questioned why he had done this, he answered, "For your privacy, Madame." She shrugged and opened the bag. But instead of resting her gaze on the delicate flower she was anticipating, she saw a very different sight—a box of sanitary napkins. Horrified, she ordered him out of the room.

How could such a misunderstanding take place? Far from the glowing lights of Las Vegas and back in Kendigelen's homeland of Turkey, Orchid is the brand name used by Procter & Gamble to market the product known as Always in the United States. In most parts of Asia, from China to Pakistan, the product is sold under the name Whisper. In Italy, it's marketed as Lines, and in Spain under the names Evax and Ausonia. When the call came in at 11 p.m., he assumed that the guest's request related more to a biological need than merely an aesthetic one. Thankfully, Kendigelen's supervisor stepped in to explain what had happened. When the guest learned the true reason for the botched delivery, she erupted with good-natured laughter.

Seventeen years later, as Kendigelen recounts the story, it's obvious that he understands the difference that a single word can make for a guest at the Bellagio. Today, he is the executive director of guest services. He oversees all of the areas where multilingual staff are of key importance—from the front desk to the valet to the box office.

"Bellagio employees speak forty-eight different languages," Kendigelen explains, holding up a twenty-nine-page list of staff members with skills in languages as diverse as Amharic, Ilocano, Lithuanian, Malayalam, and Navajo. The roster not only says which languages each employee speaks, but whether they can read and write in those languages, too. "For the languages we don't staff internally, we have twenty-four/seven access to interpreters via telephone for nearly two hundred languages," he explains. In the previous year, the hotel used the phone-based interpreting service on sixty-eight hundred separate occasions—an average of nearly twenty times each day.

Perhaps in part due to his firsthand experience with the orchid-seeking guest, Kendigelen doesn't take language for granted in his role at the Bellagio today. However, even that linguistic misunderstanding had a happy ending, creating a lifelong relationship between him and his customer. "She has been coming back to the hotel as a personal guest of mine for the last seventeen years," he points out with a chuckle. "And she loves telling people the orchid story."[16]

Domo Arigato, Mr. Auto

Let's travel now to a very different hotel, one that's located far from the bright lights of Las Vegas. Upon arrival, a young Japanese woman by the name of Izumi greets you. As you check in, she hands you a Japanese newspaper and a card with instructions to make international calls. Once you get to your room, you remove your shoes and change into slippers, just in time for the bellboy to bring you some hot green tea. After a good night's sleep, you wake up and head downstairs for the hotel breakfast, which of course, in the traditional Japanese style, consists of rice, soup, and other traditional Japanese food. There's just one catch. You're not in Japan. You're in Michigan.

Back in the 1980s, waves of Japanese businessmen started to arrive in Detroit, the automotive capital of the world. Many hotels noticed an increase in the number of these newcomers, but one local hotel, part of the Sheraton chain, was lucky enough to have an employee, Izumi Suzuki, who spoke Japanese and was able to help with the language barrier. "I translated menus. I translated phone dialing instructions. I translated many things to make their stay more comfortable," she recalls.[17]

But translation was not enough. Suzuki was the only person on the hotel staff who spoke Japanese and understood the culture. She knew she was dealing with a very specific demographic: *Japanese. Engineer. Male. Works for an automotive company. Does not know how to cook. Is far from home.* "The case with Japanese visitors was different from that of Chinese or Korean people who came here to stay," Suzuki points out. "For the Japanese, they knew they would only be staying for four or five years and would then be returning home." As a result, they often arrived with no English whatsoever.

Suzuki often found herself in the role not just of translator, but of cultural adviser. She would even receive phone calls from former guests asking her, "How do I get a driver's license?" She sometimes got called to the airport to help people find their way around. "Back then, the airport was not easy to navigate. People would frequently arrive from Japan, get lost, and miss their connecting flights." Eventually, she and some colleagues translated all of the signs that appear in the more modern airport that Detroit boasts today, but at that time, things were chaotic.

But Suzuki brought calm to the madness by helping Japanese businesspeople feel as if they had a taste of Japan in the heartland of America. Making them feel truly at home was not an easy task. To help the hotel chefs learn how to make a Japanese breakfast, she needed to show them not only how to prepare the food, but exactly where to place the rice bowl and how to position the soup for it to be served properly. For many weeks, she had to arrive each day at 5:30 a.m. until she was sure that the chefs had mastered the details.

Her work paid off. "People from Mazda would drive one hour just to come to our hotel," she recalls. The success of the hotel led it to be profiled in the *Chicago Tribune* and *New York Times*.[18] Competitor hotels tried to copy some of her ideas. "Many other hotels tried to offer a Japanese breakfast, but because they did it without authenticity, they failed," she points out. "Some hotels did not even use real Japanese rice," she scoffs. "Japanese people are very particular with rice. It has to be done the right way, or they will never go back."

In short, you don't have to own one of the world's biggest or most luxurious hotels to accommodate your guests in other languages. But you do have to pay close attention to your target market to understand how to make them feel truly welcome, from both a linguistic and a cultural perspective.

Don't Believe Everything You Can't Read

There are also times when foreign visitors wear out their welcome, and we're not just referring to the stereotypical ugly American tourist overseas. Picture this scene: The crowd scatters as the commandeered rickshaw speeds erratically down the clogged street, narrowly missing street vendors selling fried peanuts and rice wine, tipping over a cart full of polyester blouses. "*Spaß muss sein!* (You gotta have fun!)" chortles the driver, an inebriated German surgeon vacationing in China. Close behind him sprints his tour guide and interpreter, trying in vain to grab the handlebars before a passerby becomes a drive-by victim. "*Dui bu qi, dui bu qi!*" he calls out to locals between heaving breaths. "I'm sorry," he says. "So sorry."

Unfortunately, that breathless tour guide was me, Jost. When I worked as a tour guide in China for several years during the late 1980s and into the 1990s, my German-speaking tourists tended to be shy about their communication skills. It wasn't that they lacked an adventurous spirit, as the drunken example I just described makes clear. Many German tourists were highly experienced travelers who made good use of their annual six-week vacation to check off a bucket list of destinations that inevitably included China. But at the time, China still seemed mysterious and secluded. Not only that, but the Chinese language seemed so truly foreign that it tended to stifle any sense of linguistic adventure.

Even the common hand signals these veteran travelers had used elsewhere in the world were not foolproof in China. Ordering two beers the German way (holding up the thumb and the index finger) meant *eight* beers in Chinese. (Chinese number gestures allow you to show any number between zero and nine with one hand. These signals are used to bridge the many different pronunciations of numbers in Chinese dialects and to allow for a more private form of bargaining away from public sight. The gesture for eight is derived from the character for eight: 八.) The splitting headaches tourists had as a result of this miscommunication permanently destroyed any desire to communicate on their own. From that point on, as their tour guide, I had to interpret *everything*, including the 2:00 a.m. demands to move to a new hotel room because of a dripping faucet, the temper tantrums at the lack of a television in the room (in places with no reception to begin with), and even encounters with medical professionals.

Chinese medicine holds a mystical fascination for many Westerners, and my tour guests seemed to have a childlike, implicit trust that whatever they purchased in a Chinese pharmacy would be beneficial. One genteel lady with particularly bad eczema shared a common German aversion to the standard Western hydrocortisone prescription she'd been recommended in Europe, so she was so thrilled when I took her to a Chinese pharmacy and found a medication that improved her condition dramatically within a single day. I had told the pharmacist that she wanted traditional Chinese medicine, but after seeing her miserable skin condition, he gave her, yes, hydrocortisone.

I didn't read the accompanying explanations when she made her first purchase. Only later, after purchasing ten more packages of this wonder balm for the same lady during my next trip to China, did I study the packaging a little more closely on the flight back to Frankfurt and realize that she had been using hydrocortisone all along. I wanted to tell her, but when I saw her waiting for me at the gate with such great anticipation and fervent belief in the powers of Chinese medicine, the thought of disappointing her and ruining the excitement over her "miracle cure" made me change my mind. For years, the dear lady wrote to me each Christmas to thank me for her beautifully smooth skin. Is ignorance truly bliss? In this case, I like to think so.

CHAPTER 4

Sharing Stories and Spreading Religion in Translation

To read is to translate,
for no two persons' experiences are the same.

—W. H. Auden,
Anglo-American poet

Starving Artists

Literary translation is one of the most challenging types of translation work. If anyone can attest to this fact, it's Linda Asher.[1] An award-winning translator from French into English, she brought us English versions of works by such writers as Milan Kundera, Victor Hugo, and Georges Simenon. But in her day job as fiction editor at the *New Yorker*, she has also worked closely with writers in another capacity—as their editor. This gives her a unique perspective, one that encompasses all major aspects of the writing process. As Linda explains, translation can be even more challenging than writing due to the lack of flexibility afforded in translation. The translator must say exactly what the writer has said. "If the word that I've chosen has a slightly different angle and skews the entire paragraph, I have to go back and get the right word," she explains. Writers, on the other hand, can change and rewrite their sentences at will.

Contrast the level of skill required with this harsh reality: The person who translates the bestselling literary masterpieces would probably earn more working on a factory assembly line. Yes, it might be surprising, but the people who translate the ingredients on the packaging for your toilet paper earn more than those who translate the works of the greatest poets. Most people would agree that translating literature is truly an art. The phrase *starving artist* could not be more appropriate. There is very little glamour or money in literary translation, for all but a minuscule percentage of the pool.

"Most literary translators are on the verge of poverty," explains Martin de Haan, president of CEATL (the Conseil Européen des Associations de Traducteurs Littéraires or European Council of Literary Translators' Associations).[2] CEATL is Europe's leading association for literary translation, with an estimated ten thousand translators represented among its thirty-two member associations.[3] "In many countries, it is simply impossible to make a living as a professional literary translator," de Haan points out; because their income potential is so low, most literary translators also work in other professions—as teachers, university professors, writers, or journalists. Some also do technical or commercial translation work to make ends meet.

Just how poorly remunerated are literary translators? It depends on where they live. CEATL published a study showing that literary translators earned less than 50 percent of the per capita gross domestic product (GDP). In a slightly different light, the average earning power of a literary translator was inferior to the average wages in manufacturing and services in *every single country* analyzed. Indeed, in the vast majority of countries, translators earned less than 66 percent of this amount.[4] In addition, translators' names don't typically appear on the covers of the books they translate. In their day jobs, as professors, writers, and journalists, at least they would be more likely to get attribution where it is due—not so for their translation work. De Haan echoes that: "Generally speaking, translators tend to be systematically overlooked as authors."

Where might the fate of literary translators be a bit different? Perhaps in markets where reading for pleasure is a more recent phenomenon. Take the example of Sudhir Dixit, who translated the Harry Potter novels into Hindi with Manjul Publishing House. Owing in part to his translation, the first book by J. K. Rowling sold forty thousand copies, quite an impressive number for fiction sales in India. On the heels of this success, Dixit was profiled in many of the most prominent local newspapers, discussing the particulars of translation, such as his choices to use Sanskrit as a basis for spells that in English were based on Latin or Greek.

Unfortunately for translators, the Harry Potters of this world are few and far between. It remains to be seen whether literary translators will be better off in the new world of digital media and electronic book publishing.

Translating Lord Voldemort

There have been authorized translations of the Harry Potter books into at least seventy languages, and the number of unauthorized ones probably rivals that. One interesting challenge for every Potter translator is how to render the name of "Tom Marvolo Riddle." As an anagram for "I am Lord Voldemort," the name conveys an essential clue to the identity of the story's main villain. While the translators of the nonalphabetic East Asian languages had to revert to explanatory notes, translators of other languages tried to outdo each other in their creative solutions. Some languages simply modified the middle name to arrive at a comparable anagram. For instance, the Bulgarian Том Мерсволуко Риддъл (Tom Mersvoluko Riddal) is an anagram of Тук съм и Лорд Волдемор ("Here I am—Lord Voldemort"). Other translators made more complex manipulations to the name. One extremely clever solution is the French version, Tom Elvis Jedusor. Not only is this an anagram of *Je suis Voldemort* ("I am Voldemort"), but "Jedusor" is pronounced similarly to the French *Jeu du sort* (meaning "fate riddle").

Translation on the Orient Express

Dame Agatha Mary Clarissa Christie (née Miller), better known as Agatha Christie, is one of the most famous writers of all time. Her mystery novels, famous for their slow and deliberate prose and heavy doses of psychological suspense, are often listed as suggested reading in schools around the world, even in places far-removed from the scenes of British society that featured so prominently in her books.

Because her novels are so popular, publishers love to release them in other languages, and translators have historically been eager to translate them too. In Thailand alone, more than twenty translators have converted Christie's whodunits into Thai. Unfortunately, in one instance, the confusion over who had the right to publish a translation led not to a mystery exactly, but to an intellectual property lawsuit that took nearly a full decade to resolve.

According to Janine Yasovant, who reported on the court case from Thailand, Christie's British publisher held the copyrights for her works and sued the local Thai publisher for selling and reprinting the translated novel of Agatha Christie, claiming that they had violated international copyright laws. Book distribution was suspended and nearly five thousand books were seized through a court order.[5]

However, when the case was finally concluded, the court found that the defendant did not in fact violate the law. Why not? After nearly ten years of legal proceedings, the court ruled that the translators had the right to translate the book without obtaining permission from the plaintiff. The local Thai publisher was not aware that publishing the translated works would violate the copyrights. According to the courts, the defendant did not have any intention to violate the law, but many were surprised by the outcome. The original publisher would have easily won such a lawsuit in many countries. However, each country has different laws around translation and intellectual property.

Copyright issues related to translation can be so complex that they seem to warrant the skills of Hercule Poirot. In general, a translator holds the copyright to his or her work. However, translations are generally considered to be derivative works. If the translation is not authorized or licensed by the holder of the original works, it is usually deemed as an infringement. In other words, the translator's copyright is usually not independent.

But the plot thickens. If a translation is published in a country that follows the Berne Convention, copyright protection extends to fifty years after the author's death.[6] Many countries have adopted even longer terms. For example, Japan sets the term at the life of the author plus seventy-five years. That might sound relatively straightforward, but things can get trickier when a book is published in multiple countries simultaneously. A translator must look at where the book was published and determine which international agreements are followed by each country—including any bilateral agreements—before translating a single word.

In other words, being fluent in two languages is often insufficient to translate literary works. There's often a third language in which fluency is required: Legalese.

Lítost in Translation

The Czech author Milan Kundera is known for being very particular about his translations. Given that he himself was deeply involved in his own translation between Czech and French, that may not be surprising. In fact, Kundera's *Book of Laughter and Forgetting* questions the concept of translation itself: "*Lítost* is an untranslatable Czech word. Its first syllable, which is long and stressed, sounds like the wail of an abandoned dog. As for the meaning of this word, I have looked in vain in other languages for an equivalent, though I find it difficult to imagine how anyone can understand the human soul without it" (translation by Aaron Asher). Some describe it as a combination of grief, sympathy, remorse, and longing, but Kundera's translators wisely followed the author's instructions and left *lítost* untranslated.

Pick a Name, Any Name

Denys Johnson-Davies has a different take on the translator's role in writing literature. He is the most well known and prolific Arabic-into-English literary translator as well as the first translator into

English of the works of another Nobel Prize winner, Egyptian author Naguib Mahfouz.

When he was working on the translation of Mahfouz's *Conjurer Made off with the Dish*, Johnson-Davies came to the final paragraph and could not make sense of the meaning. He asked an Egyptian friend for help, but the friend was equally stymied. Finally he called Mahfouz himself, and the author admitted that the printers had omitted an entire line of essential text in the story's conclusion. Johnson-Davies was the first to notice the omission.[7]

It's not an isolated experience for Johnson-Davies, who is quick to point out that the blame lies squarely with the young and inexperienced Arabic publishing industry, which he believes is not as well staffed with editors as it should be. However, even authors are not immune to the general prevailing sloppiness. While translating a short Mahfouz novel called *The Journey of Ibn Fattouma*, a sort of Egyptian *Pilgrim's Progress*, he realized that the hero's name abruptly changes in the middle of the book. Again he called Mahfouz, who seemed amused at his discovery.

"So which name shall I call him?" Johnson-Davies asked.

"Choose whichever you like best," Mahfouz replied with a laugh.

Though the author's apathy may have frustrated Johnson-Davies, he still recommended him as the premier Arabic author when the Nobel Prize committee representative came calling for a short list of nominees. It's a revealing story of the extraordinary cultural power wielded by a translator, even though, as Johnson-Davies often bemoans, "Translation is real hard work. It's also not appreciated."[8]

The One Who Catches Hearts

J. D. Salinger's famous novel *The Catcher in the Rye* sold sixty-five million copies worldwide. Like any popular book, it was translated into multiple languages, but its title was adapted in some cases. In Sweden, it was called *Savior in a Crisis* (*Räddaren i nöden*), while in Iceland, it was *Savior in the Grass* (*Bjargvætturinn í grasinu*). The Danes went in another direction, translating it as *Damned Youth* (*Forbandede Ungdom*), and in Hungarian it became a *Sharpener of Oats* (*Zabhegyező*). In Spanish, it was rendered as *The Hidden Hunter* (*El Cazador Oculto*). In Dutch there are three translations: *Adolescent* (*Puber*), *The Catcher in the Grain* (*De vanger in het graan*), and *New York's Child Savior* (*De kinderredder van New York*). And the most romantic rendition? *The Heart Catcher* (*L'attrape-coeurs*). Leave it to the French.

Green Eggs and Ham Con Salsa

> *I do not like them,*
> *Sam-I-am.*
> *I do not like*
> *green eggs and ham.*

Achieving rave reviews is no easy feat for any book. This difficulty is magnified for a translated book, and it's even more dicey for a book that many presumed to be one of the hardest-to-translate books of all. No, we're not talking about a religious manuscript or political treatise, a groundbreaking scientific tome or avant-garde experimental poetry. We're talking about the classic children's books by Theodor Seuss Geisel, aka Dr. Seuss.

What makes these books so hard to translate? Any of the millions of fans who grew up with them can tell you: Their succinct, peculiar, and unique poetic rhythms; the many invented words and even letters; and the plays on words that twist and turn until a new meaning simply pops out from the page.

Dr. Seuss's sparkling and exciting language makes the story almost secondary. The words themselves fizzle and sizzle, capturing our imagination. Is that translatable? This became an essential question for Aida Marcuse, an experienced children's author and translator with more than fifty children's books under her belt.[9] She was handpicked by an American publisher to translate *Green Eggs and Ham* into Spanish for the U.S. market.

Aida plunged into the translation but became stuck almost immediately, poring over the book, desperately trying to find a key to the rhythm of the text. In her despair, she called her adult daughter, who had listened to her mother read the book aloud to her as a child and who had gone on to become a poet and a published children's book author.

After a bit of reflection, Aida's daughter shared a revelation: "Mom, the keyword is *Sam*, because it rhymes with *ham*. In Spanish we need a name that rhymes with *jamón*. How about *Ramón*?" Thus *Sam I am* became *Juan Ramón*. With this cornerstone in place, it took Aida all of four hours to translate the rest of the book. As sometimes happens, the translation simply flowed from there with everything falling naturally into place, even Dr. Seuss's quirky words and odd rhythms. "With the keywords in my hand," Aida said, "it all felt natural." And she knew she could make it work for Spanish-speaking readers.

Her readers agree. Up to the present day, they have bought more than 150,000 copies of *Huevos verdes con jamón*. The reviews are ecstatic, raving overwhelmingly about the success of Aida's translation rather than about the book itself.[10] Building on this initial success, Aida went on to translate other Dr. Seuss books. However, two of these—*Oh, the Places You'll Go!* and *The Lorax*—proved to be far less magical labors. In fact, they took her more than a year to translate.

The difference? Unlike *Green Eggs and Ham*, these two books, written by an aging, perhaps less inventive Dr. Seuss, didn't send Aida off on a rhythm- and language-based whirlwind. They lacked a key that would unlock the secret. Instead, the translations required intense mental effort to coin new terms and create new language, all with a young audience in mind that is no less critical than their adult counterparts. One test reader, the six-year-old bilingual granddaughter of Aida's friend in the United States, read one of the translations aloud to Aida. Aida noticed that the girl hesitated as she read two terms, so she asked whether she actually knew the terms—the terms were *tientan* (tempt) and *ni por asomo* (no way), both common terms but not familiar enough for bilingual Hispanic kids growing up in the States. "Well," was the answer, "I do, but I don't really know what they mean." So Aida went back to the text again, rewriting for clarity as well as cadence.

According to Aida, successful children's book translation is having children "read it to you and look at their eyes and look at their response. This is how you can know whether you're successful or not." And whether it's produced by one afternoon's inspired creative flow or months and months of intense intellectual effort, Aida has found a successful formula, indeed.

> *¡Me gustan mucho,*
> *mucho, mucho,*
> *los huevos verdes con jamón!*
> *¡Gracias, gracias,*
> *Juan Ramón!*

Bejuco Daydreams

A little girl stands deep in the heart of the Amazon rain forest, gazing up at a labyrinth of climbing vines. The young girl is part of the Shuar community, an indigenous group that has lived in the jungle since pre-Incan times. And these climbing bejuco are not just any vines. She and her friends play games using the bejuco, climbing them like ladders up the towering trees to watch the birds flying near the treetops. Villagers use the bejuco to build their homes, to heal, and to decorate. The bejuco is a pathway to visit the *yaa nua*, the star women who live in the sky. To this little Shuar girl, the bejuco is heavenly—beautiful and somewhat magical. So how do you translate the word *bejuco*?

The answer is found in an unlikely place, thousands of miles away in a drastically different setting—central London. Traditional black cabs whiz through the streets. Historic buildings and subway stops provide an ongoing exchange of commuters and students. Neon lights from restaurants, bookstores, and shops light up the footpath. At first glance, the only thing it has in common with the

Amazon is that it's raining. But walk into the Royal Academy of Dramatic Arts building, head upstairs and peer into the conference room, and you'll soon learn why this group is well suited to find the perfect translation.

The unlikely team includes a Finnish poet and translator with a PhD in Swahili poetry, a former British diplomat who lived and worked in China for many years, an Italian translator of West Indian francophone poetry, a physician and former editor of the *British Medical Journal*, a senior lecturer in Somali and Amharic, a Canadian feminist who works as a radio producer for the BBC, an Indian doctor and director of a Hindi publishing company, and an award-winning British poet and veteran of poetry translation who will lead the group to make the best possible choices. In total, there are ten people assembled. And none is fluent in Shuar—there are only about thirty thousand people who speak the Shuar language, and most of them live in the Ecuadorian Amazon.

As they sit around the table, their steaming cups of English tea remain largely untouched. The prospect in front of them is much more tantalizing. It's a poem—a thirteen-word poem—and their mission is to translate it into English before the evening is over. With just thirteen words, how hard could it be? That depends. *Bejuco* is just one word in the poem, but it's an essential one. And poetry translation is not exactly a straightforward process.

The path to rendering the poem into English started with the poet herself, María Clara Sharupi Jua, a Shuar woman from Ecuador, who first translated her poem from Shuar into Spanish. While Shuar is her native tongue, she's also perfectly fluent in Spanish and writes in both languages. Another attendee at tonight's meeting, a native English speaker and Spanish translator who used to live in Ecuador, has prepared some rough translations, known as "literals," that the group will use as a basis for discussion. She has carefully annotated these translations with alternate words and footnotes on cultural context. The group has already read them in advance of tonight's session.

The organization is known as the Poetry Translation Centre, and was established in 2004 by the poet Sarah Maguire to translate contemporary poetry from Africa, Asia, and Latin America and to bring these works to the English-speaking world. Under Maguire's supervision, the Poetry Translation Centre has conducted workshops to translate from languages as diverse as Assamese, Gujarati, Indonesian, Kurdish, Siraiki, Tajik, and Zapotec.[11]

As the session unfolds, the group discusses each word of the poem in painstaking detail. To do so, they use the literal translation of the poem and the Spanish version, which is read aloud at the start so everyone can hear the music of the poem. Perhaps surprising, they have the most heated debates not about the word *bejuco* but about the word *delgado*, which, when literally translated, means "thin," and is used in the poem to describe the girl's legs. However, the word *thin* does not seem to be in keeping with the spirit of this little girl's daydreams of power and adventure. The feminist in the group rightly points out that *thin* can be associated with weakness, whereas this girl seems to want to run and play. Eventually, the group chooses a more appropriate synonym, *lean*, instead.

So what did the group decide to do with the word *bejuco*? As the poet Sarah Maguire points out, "*Bejuco* is a beautiful word. There's nothing like it in English. We don't need to translate it. It can stand on its own." The group nods in unanimous agreement, reflecting on the sounds the word makes when spoken aloud and electing to add the word *vine* in order to make its meaning clear. See the results for yourself:

Dreams

By María Clara Sharupi Jua

She is five years old and daydreams
her legs are like a lean bejuco vine

The original Shuar reads: *Ewej uwi takakiat, nua uchi nuyá kará-*
meawai / makuinkia káapia anin ayat; the literal version is *She is*
five years old and daydreams / that her legs resemble a thin, climbing
bejuco vine.[12]

Where poetry translation is concerned, sometimes two, three,
or ten heads are truly better than one. Even if not all of those heads
can understand the source language, knowing the language of
poetry—and having diverse viewpoints involved in the process—is
sometimes even more important.

A Piano Sonata Played on a Trombone

In many ways, translating poetry is like playing music. First, you
must be able to read the score to understand the original composition. But if the poet's instrument is language, then each poem is
designed specifically for that instrument. Thus converting a poem
into another language is like trying to play a piano sonata on a trom-
bone. The melody of the poem may be recognizable in any language,
but its sound will be completely different once it's translated.

It takes a fine and discerning ear. Often it takes another poet.
Fortunately for us, these poet-translators are also able to clearly ar-
ticulate both the importance and the difficulty of the poetry translation task itself. Charles Simic, a Pulitzer Prize winner for poetry
and former U.S. poet laureate, immigrated to the United States from

Yugoslavia and did not begin to speak English until he was fifteen years old. For more than fifty years, in addition to writing his own poetry, he translated poems from various eastern European languages, resulting in thirteen books of translated works.

In his final appearance as poet laureate, he gave a talk at the Library of Congress in which he emphasized the value of translation to society at large. "Every culture in the world is enriched by another country's literature," Simic said. "Translators were the first multiculturalists, looking at other languages and other traditions and finding something that they wanted to translate and share."

Simic went on to explain that translating poetry is ultimately an "act of love, an act of supreme empathy." He pointed out that even when he taught literature, he never read poems as closely and meticulously as he did when translating them. He commented, "Translating is like being a medium, standing in the shoes of the person you're translating; one becomes another. It is the closest possible reading of a literary text."

Of course, because of its extreme difficulty, some go so far as to say that to even attempt to translate poetry is not only futile, but impossible. Simic disagrees: "Poetry itself is about the impossible. All arts are about doing the impossible. That's their attraction. How does a poet take an experience, big or small, and convert it into fourteen lines? But it's done."[13]

Finding Jesus (and God) in Chinese

There's an unofficial continuum of difficulty in the world of translation. The easy side begins with finding words for the tangible things that surround us, the physical objects we can see and hear and touch, those basic vocabulary words we learn in a beginning language class. As words and ideas become more complex and abstract, translation becomes more difficult. Transferring religious texts into another language can be a veritable minefield.

Take this example: the Nestorians were a Christian group that was declared heretical by the early Christian church. Back in the early seventh century, when the Nestorian missionaries went from Persia to China, they unpacked their bags and immediately began to translate and author texts in Chinese. The problem? They had not been there long enough to fully grasp the Chinese language. They needed help, so it seemed logical to ask the Buddhist monks, who were already well versed in religious terminology.

But the Nestorian missionaries apparently didn't realize that their Buddhist assistants would convey central Christian messages by using terms that were inseparably associated with Buddhism. For example, the Buddhists translated the word *God* by using *fo* (佛), which is the Chinese term for "Buddha." Similarly, for the term *Christian disciple*, they used *aluohan* (阿羅漢), which means "Buddhist spiritual practitioner." To confuse—or clarify—matters further, the Chinese terms are phonetic transcriptions of the original Sanskrit terms for *Buddha* (बुद्ध) and *Arhat* (अर्हत).[14]

The Nestorian Christians might have passed off these mistranslations as sincere attempts to find spiritual words for spiritual matters, but the transcription of the term *Jesus* revealed a certain sense of humor, if not outright sabotage. Due to the relative scarcity of syllables available in Chinese, it's possible to use a multitude of different characters (each of which stands for the same-sounding syllable) to phonetically transcribe a single foreign word. (See the story on the transcription of Coca-Cola in Chapter 5.) Because there are so many to choose from, a translator usually tries to pick characters with a descriptive or positive meaning. But the word that the Buddhist translators chose for Jesus was *yishu* (移鼠), which means "to move rats." The modern Chinese transcription for Jesus, *Yesu* (耶稣), is more clever and more fitting. According to Chinese name-giving customs, the first syllable of the transliteration of Jesus is the family name *Ye*, which *Yesu* shares with the Chinese Jehovah, *Yehehua* (耶和華). *Su*, the second syllable and Chinese given name of *Yesu*, has a number of meanings, one of which is "revive." The name is thus a play on *Yesu* as the resurrected son of God, while at the same time transliterating the sound of Jesus.[15]

But not all translations of important terms for Christian concepts have such a lighthearted ending as the translation of the word *Jesus*. In fact, one translation of God's name may have resulted in the deaths of twenty million people. The translator in question was a British missionary by the name of Robert Morrison. His translation inadvertently influenced the Taiping Heavenly Kingdom movement, which ended in 1864 after fourteen years of conflict and a bloodbath across several provinces. It's a frightening tale of unintended consequences that has haunted many religious translators.

Morrison finished the first translation of the Chinese Bible in China in 1822. For the New Testament, Morrison and his assistants, most of whom were Chinese, relied on a partial New Testament translation of Catholic origin. But for the Old Testament, they had to start from scratch. Many occurrences of God's name in the Old Testament were transliterated into English as Jehovah. Morrison accordingly transliterated this into Chinese as *Yehuohua* (爺火華), and he chose characters meaning "old man/father," "fire," and "bright."

In 1836, a failed imperial Chinese scholar named Hong Xiuquan was given a Christian tract based on Morrison's translation that included the term for Jehovah. Shortly afterward, Hong experienced a nervous breakdown that he later identified as a vision. In the vision, he described "a man venerable in years (corresponding with *ye* 爺), with golden (corresponding with *huo* 火 and *hua* 華) beard and dressed in a black robe." This image was likely inspired by the transliteration of *Jehovah* in the very first sentence of the tract. This term became a key part of the Taiping ideology—both *Yehuohua* as the personal name for God and *Ye* (爺) as "God the Father" later appeared in Taiping writings. Convinced that he was the younger brother of Jesus, Hong set up the Taiping Heavenly Kingdom and fomented violent rebellion based on his pseudo-Christian beliefs for the next decade and a half.[16]

How much responsibility should the early Bible translators bear for this bloody time span in history? Surely no single translator is to blame. Perhaps the results would have been the same, no matter what term Morrison and his coworkers had chosen. Though it's not for us to judge, the perceived burden was immense, and it may help to explain why further discussions on the translation of a term like *God* into Chinese have not been solved to the present day. The debate over the translation of the Protestant Christian concept of God into Chinese started in the early 1800s and raged in China for nearly a century, swirling around intricate theological arguments about whether the term *God* should be translated as *Shangdi* (上帝), which means "Lord on High" and was used in the old Chinese classics, or *Shen* (神), which means "spirits" or "gods," a term that would be coined especially for the Christian scriptures with little accompanying religious or cultural baggage.

The arguing parties battled passionately over whether the Judeo-Christian God had already been intrinsically known to the China of antiquity—as revealed in the myriad meanings embedded in the term *Shangdi*—or whether China's religious history, though burdened with a plethora of religiously laden terms, had never been exposed to monotheism, in which case God needed a fresh start with *Shen*. From today's viewpoint these may seem like frivolous arguments, but for the missionaries involved in these conflicts they were of vital importance. After all, at issue was whether traditional Chinese religious practices were to be condoned or condemned, whether the new religion was actually not new but something that just needed to be revived, or whether the missionaries even had a right to be in China in the first place. In short, the translation of that single word was a very big deal. [17]

Even today you can find different *Shen* and *Shangdi* editions of the Chinese Bible, but unlike the missionaries, both terms live side by side quite peacefully. In fact, many contemporary Chinese theologians argue that Chinese Christians are uniquely privileged to have both terms to express a manifold nature of God. According to this view, one of the terms represents a concept of divine immanence (*Shen*), while the other represents transcendence (*Shangdi*). To avoid complicating matters further, we focused here on the Protestant tradition only. Catholics had a similar discussion and came up with yet another term that is used in Catholic Bibles today: *tianzhu* (天主), meaning Lord of Heaven.[18]

These stories shed a fascinating light on the role of the translator. Is the translator simply a faceless and impartial converter of languages? Faceless perhaps, but certainly not impartial. And definitely not a mere converter of languages. Languages are living, breathing entities that can be formed into virtually any shape or form that a translator wants them to inhabit. And if this is true for the tangible world, it is multiplied exponentially with intangibles such as religion.

To Err Is Saintly

One of the most popular saints in art history is St. Jerome, who also happens to be the patron saint of translators. Jerome's popularity is not surprising. His life included many fairy tale–like religious traditions, such as a lion that guarded him after Jerome removed a thorn from his paw. In his real life as a theologian and Bible scholar, he managed to make enemies with most everyone he encountered. Perhaps most important, he was a prolific late fourth- and early fifth-century translator.

Before beginning his translation of the Old Testament, he studied Hebrew, the original language of most of the Old Testament books. This sounds logical, but it was far from normal in Jerome's era. The young Christian church had relied on Latin translations from a Greek version of the Old Testament, the Septuagint, a third-century BCE Jewish translation. Both Jews and Christians considered the Septuagint inspired, so a new translation of the original Hebrew source was considered not just unnecessary but unwelcome. In fact, most of Jerome's Hebrew instructors gave him lessons in secret, fearing their synagogues' disapproval.

But a little public censure never stopped Jerome from pursuing his mission. His writings reveal his understanding of the importance of translating from the original source text, regardless of the political climate. He forged ahead, reveling in the expected criticism, and his translations ended up making up most of the Latin Vulgate Bible. The Vulgate became the primary Latin Bible that is still used by much of the Catholic church to the present day. Ironically, it also served as the source text for most Catholic translations into other languages into the twentieth century, something that Jerome would have vehemently opposed.

Jerome managed to make himself equally unpopular with Christians and Jews. One passage in the Old Testament (Exodus 34:29) mentions the radiance of Moses's head as he descends from Mount Sinai. The Hebrew word for "radiance" is קָרַן or *karan*. However, Jerome was working with a version of the Hebrew text without the little diacritical marks that signify the vowels, known as niqquds. As a result, he mistranslated קרן (*k-r-n*) as "horned" (קֶרֶן, *keren*). The unfortunate Latin text says: *"cumque descenderet Moses de monte Sinai tenebat duas tabulas testimonii et ignorabat quod cornuta esset facies sua ex consortio sermonis Dei"* (underscore added to the word *cornuta*, which means *horned*).[19] The newly revised version of the Vulgate corrected this, but sadly it was not widely embraced by the Catholic church.

In the years that followed, Jerome's mistake led to many artistic depictions of Moses with horns, including a famous statue by Michelangelo and a relief in the chamber of the U.S. House of Representatives. Even more unfortunately, the anti-Semitic stereotype of Jews with horns is also most likely due to Jerome's mistranslation.

So how does it square up—this cantankerous old academic as the patron saint of translators? Well, we translators—like everyone else—are far from perfect. Many of us could even be called cranky (that's what you get from working alone most of the time). But like Jerome, most of us do dedicate our lives to researching and trying to get to the bottom of things, regardless of the personal cost, including mining the essence of the source text to be translated.[20]

When Meaning Morphs in Translation

The Hebrew phrase *tohu va vohu* (תֹהוּ וָבֹהוּ) in Genesis 1:2 originally meant formless (*tohu*) and empty or void (*vohu*), in reference to the state of things before creation. These terms also appear in Isaiah 34:11 and Jeremiah 4:23. However, the phrase eventually migrated into other languages and took on new meanings. For example, in French today, the term *tohu-bohu* means chaos or confusion. *Tohu-wabohu* in German has the same meaning, as does *tohuvabohu* in Estonian and Hungarian. Indeed, the phrase has evolved to mean chaos in modern Hebrew as well, even though the original intended meaning was clearly different. Later scholars who translated this term tried to emulate some of its original Hebrew flavor by employing rhyme, such as *Irrsal und Wirrsal* (in a 1954 German translation by Buber and Rosenzweig) or by using alliteration, such as *welter and waste* (in a recent English translation by Robert Alter). In other words, in the process of moving across languages, the meaning of *tohu va vohu* was transformed from "emptiness and nothingness" to "chaos," which many would say are complete opposites.

Scripture Translation: No Holy Book Required

It's not surprising that religious translation in the Western world tends to focus primarily on Christian translation, as exemplified by St. Jerome. But what about other religions? Do religions other than the Abrahamic "book" religions—Judaism, Christianity, and

Islam—lack scriptures to translate? Far from it. Take Buddhism, practiced today by approximately half a billion people throughout the world. Buddhism has a large multilingual following with a long history of translation that has contributed greatly to its success as a major world religion.

If not for its translations, the vast majority of Buddhist scriptures would have been lost when India's Muslim rulers destroyed many of the original Sanskrit writings in the late twelfth century. Fortunately, by that time, Buddhist monks in Tibet and China had completed major translation projects into the classical forms of Tibetan and Chinese. However, today those texts are understandable to only a select few. As a result, less than 5 percent of the Tibetan texts and only 15 percent of the Chinese texts have ever been translated into modern languages.

An ambitious new undertaking may rise to the challenge, known as the 84000 project (*84000* is an auspicious number in Buddhism, symbolizing the infinity and vastness of Buddhist teachings). The project's ambition is to translate all Buddhist scriptures from Tibetan and classical Chinese into modern languages, primarily English, within the next hundred years—a long-term goal indeed. At this point, only about 4 percent of the first of many stages is complete.[21]

It is interesting that these texts all stem from only one school of Buddhism, the Mahayana school, which already has significantly more translated material in Western languages because it has attracted the most religious interest in the West. Theravada Buddhism, the form of Buddhism followed in most of Southeast Asia, has seen significantly less translation effort. The sheer size of the task— many individual Buddhist texts are longer than the Bible—makes it too daunting to find anyone ready to commit to such a Herculean undertaking.

Buddhism expert Kate Crosby describes one reason for this slow pace of translation: After learning the minimum of four languages necessary to read the largest Buddhist canons, textual scholars often try to master up to five other regional languages to adequately access other Buddhist scholarship. By the time they've learned those languages to a sufficiently high degree, Crosby complains, their brains are simply too worn out to produce useful work.[22]

Another explanation for the story of the missing Theravada translations lies in Western stereotypes of Buddhism, which long held that the Theravada form of Buddhism was similar to the no-pomp-and-circumstance Protestantism, while Mahayana Buddhism had more in common with the mystical and mysterious Catholicism. As a result, adherents simply didn't translate scriptures unless they matched their preferred and socially accepted version of Buddhism. One kind of writing that fell under this kind of censorship included sexually explicit texts, used to describe the penalty monks had to undergo for sex-related sins. Scholars have written much about the censorship of translators and translations, but this provides a telling example of translators acting as their own censors.

Given all these problems with the translation of Buddhist texts, perhaps it's not surprising that in many monasteries in China, monks still chant Buddhist texts in Sanskrit or Pāli by relying on phonetic transliteration with Chinese characters, thus making any understanding of the text impossible. It's a remarkable similarity to the use of Latin liturgy in many Catholic churches well into the 1960s. And it's a compelling argument for the importance of translation in ensuring Buddhism's continuing survival.

Translating the Untranslatable

Is the word of God translatable? Followers of different faiths, including Islam, have found various answers to this question. Throughout history, prominent voices within the Muslim world have declared that the Koran can be *explained* only through a foreign language version rather than properly translated from Arabic. However, there have always been others who have argued for the need of translation, pointing out that there was translation even in the very beginnings of Islam.

Indeed, the sheer number of existing translations tells a story of its own. The Koran has been completely translated into more than sixty languages. There are more than forty complete published translations of the Koran into English alone, of which more than a dozen versions have come out since 2000.

Tarif Khalidi, a professor of Islamic and Arabic studies at the American University of Beirut who released an English translation in 2008, explains that in the past, there was no consensus on this question among Muslim scholars. "The arguments pro and con were both theological as well as linguistic. But nowadays this is no longer an issue," he claims. "Whatever objections might have been raised in the past are now completely transcended."[23]

But not all scholars agree with Tarif's assessment. Nazeer Ahmed, a former legislator in India and a senior U.S. scientist who was a chief engineer on the Hubble Space Telescope, also published a Koran translation in 2010. Nazeer sees his work as an expression of meaning rather than pure translation. "The Koran is the Word of God," he muses. "As such its vibrations can only be felt. It cannot be translated. Nonetheless, scholars have considered it an honor to attempt to express its meaning as they have understood it in space-time."[24]

Some of these arguments on the Koran's translatability are theological, some are linguistic, and some are aesthetic. Few people would argue that a translation—in any language—could equal the original Arabic in beauty, especially in its recited form. Witness the number of websites where you can read translated versions and listen to their recitation in Arabic at the same time.[25] Even the Koran itself addresses the topic of its transmission language: Sura 12:2 says إِنَّا أَنزَلْنَاهُ قُرْآنًا عَرَبِيًّا لَعَلَّكُمْ تَعْقِلُونَ. According to Nazeer Ahmed's translation, this means "Behold! We have revealed to you the Quran in Arabic so that you may understand."

The Koran was originally written in Arabic, and to the faithful it represents the very voice of God. But to those who don't read Arabic, the translations provide an essential accessibility. In fact, Tarif Khalidi believes that a knowledge of Arabic is no longer necessary for understanding the Koran. The many English translations allow the modern reader to reconstruct the general meaning as well as the tone and style of the original, to some extent, thus easing the entry for the Koran into the canon of the religious scriptures of humankind.

Or, in the words of two other translators of a 1997 version of the Koran, Muhammad Bāqir Behbūdī and Colin Turner: "To say that the Quran is untranslatable is not to say that it should not be translated."[26]

Giving Power to the People

A similar commitment to providing accessibility to common be-
lievers drove the prisoner Martin Luther to take up the translation
of the New Testament. Shivering in the limited winter hours of day-
light filtering into his stone cell in the bailiff's lodge at Wartburg
Castle in Eisenach, Germany, Luther picked up his quill and began
to translate. The result: 138,020 words in ten weeks—in the year
1521. Assuming a five-day workweek, he translated 2,760 words per
day, which is similar to, if not slightly higher than, the standard
daily output of the modern translator (around 2,500 words per
day). Even a present-day translator with the conveniences of modern technology would find it challenging to translate such a large
amount of completely new text so quickly. But Luther was not just
any translator.

Before his translation, the Bible was read only by the richest and
most educated members of society. Sure, Bibles were available across
Germany, but most of them could be read in Latin only. German
translations existed but were not widely accessible to the masses. It
was in the church's financial and political interests to keep the majority of the people ignorant about the Bible, making them believe,
for example, that if they wanted forgiveness for their sins, all they
had to do was pay for it.

When Luther's translation was disseminated, something remarkable happened. The common people no longer had to rely on
priests and monks to read the book on which their faith was based.
Even those who were considered lowly members of society—the
likes of shoemakers and (gasp!) women—could suddenly understand the Bible for themselves. At a time when books were scarce

and access to education was limited, literate people memorized and recited passages to others, so that those who couldn't read also benefited from the information. The number of people reading (and hearing) the New Testament in German swiftly grew.

Within a few months of Luther's translation being printed, folks from all walks of life began to discuss the Bible with priests, monks, and even highly educated masters of theology. Laypeople began to contradict and even argue with members of the clergy. Women were suddenly found holding intellectual arguments with men. The church's ability to hide behind Latin was gone. Luther's translation gave information to the masses, a powerful weapon that, combined with other factors, triggered a societal transformation.

Part of the popularity of Luther's translation was due to the language he used. The German he employed at the time seemed vibrant and modern and was more designed for the ear than for the eye. He knew that his translation would be read aloud, so he took care to make sure that the words sounded pleasant when spoken. He listened carefully to the rhythm of the language, avoiding sentences with too many unwieldy subordinate clauses and complex structures. "To translate properly is to render the spirit of a foreign language into our own idiom," he wrote. "I try to speak as men do in the market place."

For example, Luther took Matthew 12:34b and broke it into two sentences to make it easier to read aloud—and simpler to memorize and understand. The King James Version follows the Greek syntax closely: "for out of the abundance of the heart the mouth speaketh." Luther translated this verse into German as, "*Wes das Hertz vol ist, des gehet der Mund vber,*" or in English, "The person with a full heart has an overflowing mouth."

Luther himself was born a peasant, so it's no wonder he wanted to make sure that commoners—including his own family members—would be able to understand the book that he regarded as holy. Luther strove to incorporate colloquial language as well as expressions that were modern or just coming into use. Occasionally, he even coined his own terms, popularizing them in the process. Terms like *geistreich* (intelligent), *kleingläubig* (of little faith), *Machtwort* (authoritative guidance), and *Hochmut* (arrogance) are terms that were created by Luther and are still used today. To give his translation both a local and universal appeal, he embraced the entire range of the German tongue, incorporating linguistic features from as many geographic regions as possible.

Luther's translation was one of the most important influences in the history of the development of the German language. Before its publication in 1522, there was no standard language in German literature.[27] Before long, the direct and uncomplicated language of Luther's translation found its way into the pulpits and parish schools. His words became their words; his phrasing became theirs, too. The language of his translation began to surface in both scholarly writing and in the homes of peasants.

Though he translated the entire New Testament in just ten weeks, Luther took another twelve years to produce a complete translation of the entire Bible. Part of the reason it took him so long was his relentless perfectionism. Often, in search of the most intelligible word, he would spend a month talking to people in different regions. He once had the town butcher cut up sheep so that he could study their entrails and better translate sections on rites of sacrifice under Mosaic law. He made constant revisions and corrections, purging the translation of obscure or ambiguous words, painstakingly improving quality and readability, and always keeping in mind his goal of producing a text that would be rhythmic and melodious when read aloud. To improve the quality of his translations even further, he formed a translation committee, which he called a *Sanhedrin*, to ensure a translation that matched his standards for readability and a natural cadence when spoken aloud. "Translators must never work by themselves," he wrote. "When one is alone, the best and most suitable words do not always occur to him."

He even went so far as to complain that the German language was simply insufficient to express the beauty of Hebrew texts. "It is as though one were to force a nightingale to imitate a cuckoo, to give up his own glorious melody for a monotonous song he must certainly hate," he wrote. When writing about the translation into German of the book of Job, a biblical figure who was tested repeatedly by God through numerous tribulations, Luther wittily observed that the book seemed to suffer even more at the hands of the translator than Job had in his original travails.

In spite of Luther's ongoing translation misgivings, his work rescued the Bible from its place in Germany as a foreign book in a foreign tongue. The language into which he translated—not just German, but the vernacular—changed individuals' ability to not only understand their faith more deeply, but to question and reflect on it.

CHAPTER 5

Partaking in Pleasures and Delighting the Senses in Translation

An act of translation is an act of love.

—George Steiner, European-American author

Cupid Calling

There are those who love to travel, and then there are those who travel to love. Lonely, middle-aged men, often American, use international dating services to travel to foreign countries and meet women who are dreaming of a husband—and a better life abroad. When the men arrive, they are taken to events where they are introduced to groups of women interested in making a love connection. When they don't speak the same language, that's where I (Nataly) come in.

I had interpreted for this couple via telephone before. She was in Colombia, and he was in Ohio. He had visited her three times already. Many of their phone calls involved her immigration paperwork, as they were hoping to get married and he needed to bring her to the States on a fiancée visa. When couples start to get affectionate,

I find it hard to convey the same level of enthusiasm they feel for each other, but I always give it a valiant effort anyway.

But on this particular evening, they were feeling a little more frisky than normal. I was not even sure how to interpret some of the hints she kept dropping about what she wanted to do in their next encounter while retaining the same level of flirtatiousness and sexual innuendo. When I'm on these calls, I begin to understand why actors say they feel uncomfortable during sex scenes with all kinds of people watching. I feel like an intruder who has been mistakenly placed in the midst of an intimate relationship. I guess you could call it a three-way of sorts, but not the kind that fantasies are made of.

Because they were feeling amorous, they started talking about the next time they would see each other. He wanted to book a trip to see her in June, so he asked what dates would be best. "Anytime, baby," she purred. "I'll be counting down the minutes and you know what I'll be wearing." He asked again what dates would work best for his visit. "Oh, I am all yours. Every last bit of me. Any day you choose." She giggled. I had to remind myself not to interpret the giggle, feeling more than a little ridiculous repeating these words.

But he wanted an exact date. She continued saying that anytime would be fine. I interpreted essentially the same question and answer over and over, until I realized what he was really asking—or at least, I thought I knew. "Excuse me, sir, this is the interpreter speaking. Are you trying to ask what dates would be best to *avoid* for the trip?" A sigh of relief greeted my question. "Yes, interpreter, that's exactly what I am trying to find out." I interpreted this question to her with a knowing voice, hoping she would get the hint, but she still did not seem to understand. "As I said, baby, I'm yours, any day.

Or any night. Or all night." I rolled my eyes. Oh, brother. We would need to be more direct than this. I interpreted it back, nonetheless. Finally, a lightbulb appeared above his head (or below his belt): "Oh, I know, interpreter! Ask her if she remembers back in December, how there were a few days at the end of the trip when we couldn't, er, say good-bye the way we wanted to?"

I was pretty sure she was not going to understand it this time either. Even though I know I'm supposed to stay faithful to the speaker and not add anything, some situations call for an exception. After all, he is paying for the interpreting services on a per-minute basis. "Elena, do you remember back in December, when we couldn't say good-bye at the end of the trip the way we wanted to?" I added, ". . . because you were having your period?"

"Any week except the week of the twelfth," she promptly answered.

You May Kiss the #&@* Bride!

When a couple decided to have their vows renewed in the Maldives, they chose to have a traditional ceremony conducted in the local language, which they did not speak themselves. Unbeknownst to the couple, the officiant did not recite the traditional romantic vows they had hoped for. Instead, he spent the entire ceremony making insulting comments about the couple and stating that their marriage was illegitimate. The entire spectacle was later posted on YouTube—with subtitles in English.[1] Planning a vows-renewal ceremony or destination wedding in a place where you don't speak the language? Don't forget to book an interpreter!

The Language of Love

> *Lolita, light of my life, fire of my loins. My sin, my soul.*
> *Lo-lee-ta: the tip of the tongue taking a trip of three steps*
> *down the palate to tap, at three, on the teeth. Lo. Lee. Ta.*

Now, read Vladimir Nabokov's famous introductory lines again. Aloud this time. Don't listen to the meaning of the words. Just listen to their rhythm, their sounds, the way they reverberate even after you've finished reading them. That's how powerful, persuasive, and sensual language can be. The sound of every word and every syllable is placed and chosen perfectly. But can prose this pitch perfectly balanced be translated?

Here's one rendering:

> *Лолита, свет моей жизни, огонь моих чресел. Грех мой, душа моя. Ло-ли-та: кончик языка совершает путь в три шажка вниз по небу, чтобы на третьем толкнуться о зубы. Ло. Ли. Та.*

We can see its similarity, but it's difficult to evaluate its success without being able to read Russian—or at least the Cyrillic alphabet. But our Russian friends tell us that they feel the same kind of shivers and tingle of excitement when they read it.[2] In other words, even such intimate language is translatable. The passage still sounds erotic, even when translated. (Vladimir Nabokov originally wrote *Lolita* in English. He had the privilege of growing up trilingually in an aristocratic Russian family, and he also personally translated *Lo-lita* into Russian.)

Could the language itself have something to do with the text's ability to tantalize its readers? English speakers often say that French is the language of love. Or perhaps Italian. Maybe even Spanish. There's just something about those Romance languages. Russian, too, can sound quite exotic to many English speakers. But some languages just don't seem to make us want to fall in love the way others do. Take this example:

> Giselle was totaal hulpeloos in zijn armen, overgeleverd aan de storm van gevoelens die haar zo onverwacht had overmeesterd. Ze klampte zich vast aan de man die de veroorzaker was van deze storm, hopend dat ze het zou overleven. Haar lichaam was bezig zich te openen en alle muren die ze zo zorgvuldig om zich heen had opget-rokken, dreigden af te brokkelen. Het zou niet lang duren voor deze golf van sensaties vrij spel had.

Pretty hot, right? While they may not seem very romantic at first glance, the sentences above were carefully crafted with the purpose of making women swoon. They describe how the romance novel's main character, Giselle, is "totally unable to withstand the storm lashing at her, able only to cling to the man who was the cause of it and praying that she would survive whilst her body opened all its gateways and let down its barriers to admit the rolling, roiling ferocity that was now possessing her."

You can practically smell the musk of Fabio. If it sounds like the stuff of Harlequin, that's because it is. These lines come from the third chapter of the *Reluctant Surrender* by Penny Jordan, published in English by Mills and Boon, which is owned by Harlequin. It also happens to be the work of Peggy van Mossevelde, a Dutch translator who specializes in the translation of romance novels.[3] The prose of romance novels is notoriously charged with romanticism and eroticism, something that Peggy admits presents linguistic challenges: "Dutch is a much more concise and businesslike language, which is not conducive to being romantic."

The notion of romantic love is universal, and so, apparently, is the appeal of hairless pectoral muscles bulging against the backdrop of misty castles. While the covers—with their images of manly hands grasping unsheathed swords—no doubt send a message all their own, it's the stories that seduce the readers. Harlequin's books are sold in 107 countries around the world. Its more than one thousand authors publish about 120 new books per month in twenty-nine languages, including Dutch. Harlequin routinely obtains more than half its revenue from outside its home market. Because most of the authors write in English, the company depends heavily on translation.[4]

The toughest task for Peggy is adapting the novels both linguistically and culturally for Dutch-speaking readers. "I once left out a sentence about a woman being unable to live without a certain man in her life. I don't know about other countries, but I felt that Dutch women wouldn't like such an extreme degree of surrender—it would be a bit much." In summary, where erotic fiction and romance novels are concerned, coming up with the right words is not really the problem. Crossing cultures presents the most difficult challenges.

Victorian Secrets

It's one of the most popular books in the world, with millions of copies sold. Perhaps there's even one in the drawer of your bedroom nightstand. But very few people know what the title actually means. Imagine listing "sensual pleasure" as one of the three most important pursuits of your life. The word *kama* essentially means "sensual pleasure" in the context of ancient Indian Hindu tradition. The term doesn't just mean pleasure or desire—instead, it evokes a quest for pleasure, almost as if it were a sacred and spiritual duty.

Sutra is a thread or a connecting line that holds things together, or a formula. Thus one way of translating *kama sutra* (कामसूत्र in Sanskrit) would be "formulas for sensual pleasure." Many guides have been written with similar words in their titles (think the *Joy of Sex*), but no words that fit on a book cover really do justice to the concept of a lifelong commitment to seeking pleasure. At least, not in English. The most faithful and concise translation we could suggest would be something along the lines of "Enlightened Sensuality."

The eighteen-hundred-year-old book is mistakenly known throughout the Western world as a book of contortionist sexual positions. While it's true that 4 percent of the book does discuss sexual postures, its primary goal is to describe the pleasure-oriented aspects of human life. That's what the rest of the book covers— everything from how to arrange your furniture to maintaining power in a marriage. It even includes recipes for love potions that include ingredients like the bone of a camel soaked in marigold juice.

It took quite a daring and unconventional person to successfully translate the *Kama Sutra* into English for the first time. It took even more guts to publish it back in restrained Victorian times, when such writing was considered not only risqué but pornographic (even without the illustrations that would be added later). Enter Captain Sir Richard Francis Burton, who was not only a linguist, but a soldier, explorer, writer, cartographer, poet, fencer, and diplomat. With a voracious appetite for languages, he reportedly learned at least twenty-five different tongues with varying levels of fluency.[5]

When his diplomatic career was over, and as he neared the end of his life, Burton became focused on an important mission. He wanted to give English readers a more satisfying sex life. He worked with Indian scholars to translate several other Sanskrit and Arabic-language guides on the subject.

Had it not been for Burton overseeing its translation, the first into any European language, the *Kama Sutra* would likely still be unknown to English readers. The book's publication sparked debate and got people thinking about other ways to view their lives, and especially their sexuality in one of the most gender-divided and sexually conservative periods in European history.[6]

To Translate One's Longing

Many believe that one of the most beautiful words in Portuguese is *saudade*, which refers to something loved and lost. The world-famous Fado music, known for its mournful singing, is linked to *saudade*. There is no exact word for the term in English, although some would liken it to a yearning or a longing for something that is no longer attainable—more intense than nostalgia. Others have called it the love that remains after someone (or something) is gone. The word has been used to express the sadness of those who disappeared in shipwrecks as well as the longing for home the many Portuguese sailors experienced. While no perfect equivalent exists in English, the Bosnian word *sevdah* has the same complex meaning and comes from the same root.

It's a Dirty Job, but . . .

Everyone knows that sex sells, but few people know that translation often plays a part. Because of the social taboos surrounding adult entertainment, you won't find many translators who proudly display the words *porn translator* on their business cards. We interviewed several translators of adult content during the course of doing research for this book. All of them insisted that they had no ethical or moral issues with translating pornography whatsoever, but tellingly, none of them wanted to be personally identified. Yet they're out there translating XXX-rated content each and every day.

Knowing that porn consists mostly of images, you might be asking yourself, "How difficult can it be?" Rest assured, the translator's job consists of a lot more than just translating "*¡Sí! ¡Sí! ¡Sí!*" or "*Ja! Ja! Ja!*" into another language. Because a great deal of adult content is now provided on the Internet, one important area of porn translation is perhaps one of the unsexiest topics you can imagine—search engine optimization.

Yes, it's actually someone's job to translate sex-related keywords, so that when users type those words into their favorite search engine, they'll be able to find whatever fetish or scenario tickles their fancy. It might sound like fun to try to figure out how to render racy terms and phrases for a living, but it can be quite difficult. The terminology is constantly evolving, and many languages lack perfect linguistic equivalents—as in many terms from Japanese adult manga and anime.

However, use the wrong word, one that has a silly connotation or is overly euphemistic, and the meaning is lost. Like porn itself, the translation comes in various forms. Some translators get a spreadsheet with a list of keywords to translate. Others have to watch video content to subtitle or write scripts that will later be used for multilingual voice talent to overdub. And others translate the html files that appear on web pages, carefully skipping over the tags that affect the display and replacing the captions with equivalents in another language.

Because porn is so diverse, translators may feel comfortable with some types of content but not others. For example, a translator might have no qualms about subtitling hard-core films, but may refuse to translate animated pornography out of concern that it is designed for children. Other translators may feel happy to translate content related to heterosexual encounters, but not homosexual ones. Some are happy to deal with words, so long as they don't have to look at the accompanying images.

It isn't always easy to find translators willing to accept these projects, but regardless of one's own thoughts on the morality of adult content, the need to translate it isn't going to go away anytime soon.

Love Is a Battlefield

Tetsu Nakama made a living from translating love letters for more than half a century. Japanese by birth, he learned English in school after World War II ended, with the prospect of eventually gaining employment at a U.S. military base. But that changed when his cousin brought him a letter from a U.S. soldier to a bar hostess in Koza (today's Okinawa). He agreed to translate the love letter from English into Japanese.[7]

He must have had a knack, because more requests for love letter translation started pouring in. He translated in both directions, billing his clients a total of 50¢—equivalent at the time to a daily wage for a menial worker—to translate a postcard and a two-page reply. At first, he had mixed feelings about helping build relationships between U.S. soldiers and women from Okinawa. His memories of being attacked by U.S. planes as a child remained vivid. However, one letter at a time, he began to see that many women were falling in love, not just with the American men, but with the dream of a new life amid rather grim conditions. Many of them had lost their former husbands and families during the war. The bicultural relationships gave them hope of escaping not only from poverty but from painful memories.

Nakama started his business in 1957. As time passed and the Vietnam War grew in intensity, the number of requests for letters grew, and so did Nakama's business. At the height of the war, up to thirty women would visit Nakama's office per day, bearing letters from their beloved soldiers. Nakama's eyes saw letters from mothers reporting to their sons' lovers that they had been killed in battle. He also sometimes saw young women smile with delight upon reading his translations and learning that their dear boyfriends' lives had been spared.

Fifty years after Nakama translated his first letter, he was still actively translating—albeit far fewer love letters than when he first started.[8] In the Internet age, letters that go through the postal service are far less common than in the past. But the need for translation of loving written messages continues. Couples with hearts in their eyes will still defy any barrier in order to be together. That includes language.

> ### Chocolates for Japanese Men on Valentine's Day
>
> Valentine's Day in Japan was introduced by department store Morozoff Ltd. in 1936 and aimed primarily at foreigners. By 1953, Morozoff began encouraging consumers to buy heart-shaped chocolates. Candy companies soon began their own campaigns, but at one point a statement from a chocolate company executive was mistranslated, leading people to believe that women were supposed to buy chocolate for men. Japan now has a separate holiday for women on March 14, on which men buy women white chocolates, jewelry, and lingerie. But on February 14, it's the women in Japan who buy the chocolate.

XOXOXO

Of course, romantic love is not the only kind of love, nor is it the most challenging to communicate. Have you ever stood, flipping open greeting cards, one after another, in search of the perfect sentiment for a friend or loved one, only to realize that an hour has passed and you haven't found quite the right one?

Things get even more complicated when special occasions cross cultures. For example, the Hispanic concept of a fifteen-year-old girl's birthday, a *quinceañera*, celebrates not only fifteen years on the planet but a girl's transition into womanhood (it's also called a *fiesta de quince* in some parts of Latin America). In many ways, the *quinceañera* celebration has more in common with a wedding than with a birthday party. It's a very important occasion, one that's special enough to merit its own greeting card.

If you're asking yourself where on earth to buy a *quinceañera* card, it may be as easy as visiting your nearest shopping mall. Go into nearly any Hallmark store in the United States, and you'll find not only these cards, but many others that are part of the Hallmark Sinceramente line, which is designed specifically for Hispanic consumers. Hallmark has a long history of creating cards in other languages, dating back to their first card in French for the Canadian market in 1931. By the 1940s, they were selling cards in Bohemian (what is known as the Czech language today), French, German, Italian, Norwegian, Polish, Spanish, and Swedish. Today, they sell cards in more than thirty languages in a hundred countries around the globe, including bilingual cards for Hispanics in the United States.

According to a 2010 report from the U.S. Census Bureau, Hispanics make up 16 percent of the country's population, or 50.5 million people, so the demand for Spanish-language cards is immense.[9] It probably comes as no surprise that the top markets for the Hallmark Sinceramente cards are Puerto Rico, Miami, New York, Los Angeles, and Chicago. What might surprise you is that the masterminds who create the cards are based not in one of these Hispanic hubs but at the Hallmark worldwide headquarters in Kansas City, Missouri. And perhaps even more important, it's where a small but specialized bilingual and bicultural team creates the concepts for the Sinceramente line.

The editorial team has developed more than two thousand cards for the line, but it consists of just three people—Sergio Moreno, Mónica Delaorra, and Erika Garces-Alarco.[10] The work that goes into creating the cards is not considered translation, but rather *transcreation*. With transcreation, the text is not transferred from one language to another but re-created entirely. The editorial team starts not with a source text to be translated but with a concept to be conveyed. They might take a concept from one card or several. Using these ideas, they will incorporate elements from different cards and sometimes generate entirely new ones. In most cases, the transcreated cards bear little or no resemblance to the original. For example, you might find a get-well card in English that has the same image on the front as the transcreated card in Spanish, but the message may say something completely different, and the image has likely been modified as well.

However, in addition to transcreation, the Sinceramente team also does what is known as back-translation—once they come up with the verses for the cards in their target language, Spanish, they translate those expressions back into English, so that consumers who don't speak Spanish will be able to understand what they are buying. These are back-translations in another sense, too—the translations actually appear on the backs of the cards. "Just as much work goes into making sure that the back-translation carries the spirit of the Spanish," Sergio explains. The team also notes that putting the translation on the back of the card has an additional advantage—it directs people to look at the Hallmark crown logo, helping, albeit subtly, to build brand loyalty over time. After all, expressing your love for someone is serious business.

The Bold and the Beautiful

Men and women will go to great lengths to look good. That's why tourists from all over the world seek low-cost options for their tummy tucks, breast augmentations, nose reshaping procedures, and, of course, "Brazilian butt lifts," the newly popular enhancement of the gluteus maximus first popularized in Giselle Bündchen's homeland. Medical tourism is a thriving industry, with many Americans and Europeans flocking to other countries for a diverse array of beautifying cosmetic procedures.

From the minute a would-be medical tourist types the words *cheap nose job overseas* into a search engine, translation is already hard at work behind the scenes. The results that appear—in any language—depend greatly on the medical facility's online marketing. To ensure that people with fat wallets (and bodies) can find them, these businesses make sure that their websites are packed with common search terms and phrases in all the major languages.

A website's ability to reach potential customers may vary significantly from one language to the next, and even from one country to another. A British resident searching for liposuction options overseas will quickly be routed to a site in the Czech Republic. An Australian looking for a breast augmentation will likely arrive at a web property based in Thailand. People in North America in need of a tummy tuck will find medical facilities in Poland appearing on their screen. Once users get to a website, they start reading testimonials, learning more about the facility, and inquiring about the costs. However, all that web content first had to be translated from Czech, Thai, Polish, and so on into languages with large customer bases, such as English and Arabic. (Wealthy patients from Middle Eastern countries are one of the largest target markets for healthcare-related travel.)

If the shopper is having difficulty deciding which facility to choose, language becomes a critical differentiator. Facilities go to great lengths in their marketing content to alleviate patient concerns about language barriers. Many medical tourism sites reassure prospective visitors by letting them know how many bilingual doctors and nurses they have on staff, but they also specifically tout their translation and interpreting services. For example, Phuket Hospital in Thailand has interpreters for fifteen different languages.[11] Not to be outdone, Bangkok International Hospital employs seventy interpreters and boasts an internal translation center that produces marketing materials in Korean, Japanese, Khmer, Lao, and Arabic.[12] Inbound medical tourism is common too—the Mayo Clinic is one of the most popular destinations for foreign patients visiting the United States and offers a host of languages for translation and interpreting.[13]

Language work becomes even more important once a medical procedure is booked. Before the visit, insurance documents and medical records must be translated. Communications with patients—including emails and voice mails—also need to be rendered into the local language and retained in the patient's file. When the patient actually arrives at the facility, much of the written documentation has already been translated, such as discharge instructions and rehabilitation exercises. However, the patient will often rely on an interpreter to communicate with different staff members throughout the stay.

Patient-provider communications are not the only types of translated information that keeps the cosmetic-surgery industry churning. Translators routinely translate scientific papers, either to be published in international medical journals or for consumption by professionals and educators at medical schools. International conferences on cosmetic surgery require interpreters too. New innovations in the field depend on translation to apply for international patents. The machines and instruments used also require translation of technical documentation and adaptation of the electronic interfaces for local markets. So, are translators and interpreters making the world a more beautiful place? We suppose so, depending on your definition of beauty.

Cow Dung for Bouncy Curls

Hair care company Clairol launched a curling iron called the Mist Stick in the United States in 2006. The product did very well—so well that they decided to sell it in other countries, too. The problem? In German-speaking countries, the word *Mist* means "manure." It didn't sell so well in those markets. (And if you're a fan of Sierra Mist soda, now you also know why you won't find it when traveling in Germany.)

Color-Blind and Tongue-Tied

Colors are among the first things that you learn in most languages, whether you're learning natively as a child or studying a second language. So they should be the easiest things to translate, right? Not exactly. Take the Spanish word *guindo*. How to say it in English? Reddish brown? Red wine? Cranberry? Reddish purple? Burgundy? The term means "sour cherry" in Spanish, but it's difficult to come up with the exact color in English. *Cherry* on its own brings a brighter color to mind, but *dark red* doesn't quite cut it either.

Generally, one can translate a color like *guindo* by using more descriptive language instead of using a single word to translate it directly. But some languages present even greater challenges. For example, how do you translate a word that can mean either blue or green? A surprising number of languages have a word that can mean both. Linguists actually use the word *grue* to refer to this phenomenon. It's more common than you might think. Languages with small populations of speakers, like Navajo, Tzeltal, and Tarahumara, all have a word that can mean both blue and green. But even languages with millions of speakers have grue-like notions. In Vietnamese, the color word *xanh* can be used to describe either the sky or the leaves of trees. In Thai, the word เขียว means "green" but can also be used to describe the sky. In Japanese and Korean, there is not always a clear distinction between green and blue. In both languages, a green traffic light can also be called a blue light.

Not only are colors not simple to translate but they are not universal either. A language spoken in the Philippines, Hanuno'o, has words for just four colors—black, white, red, and green. Pirahã, a language of the Amazon, has no specific words to convey color but uses comparisons instead—for example, instead of saying "red," they say an item looks "like blood."

Tempted to think that a lack of words for color is somehow indicative of a "primitive" or less-developed language? Consider the fact that Latin originally had to borrow the words for *gray* and *brown* from Germanic languages. Ancient Hebrew had no word for blue. Some languages have richer palettes for certain colors than others—for example, Navajo distinguishes between the black associated with darkness and the one used for the color of coal. Spanish has many words for brown. Brown hair is *castaño*, brown skin and sugar are *moreno*, brown bears are *pardo* (the word *pardo* is sometimes described as a grayish brown in English and is also used to describe overcast skies), other brown animals are *marrón*, and yet the word *café* (same as the word for coffee) is the generic word for brown.

Conveying color words from English into other languages is not always straightforward either. Just consider the fact that black tea is known as red tea in Chinese. But we don't even have to cross languages to find examples of color confusion: white wine is not really white but pale yellow, and red wine is more of a maroon. So in many languages, the words for red and white do not appear in the translation for these wines. Also, in English, we refer to one's skin color with terms such as white and black, even though a white person's skin is not white but a pale shade of pinkish peach, and the skin we refer to as black can be many different shades of brown—not the actual color black.

So the next time you walk into your local pharmacy and see twenty different shades of hair dye for would-be redheads sitting on the shelves, consider the poor translator who has to come up with creative ways to convey "sunset auburn," "glowing auburn," "radiant auburn," "fairest auburn," and so on.

Shampoo to Promote Hair Loss

Many Americans know the Pert brand of shampoo. Before launching it in France, however, the savvy marketers changed the name to *prêt*, which means "ready." Why? The word *perte* means "loss" in French, and the company understandably wanted more favorable connotations associated with their brand.

MAC, Makeup, and Mexico

> *A lavender-lovely Fergie asks us to enter a new kind of dreamscape, to feel the "Yes, we can!" of tomorrow, and to push forward on behalf of every man, woman and child affected by HIV/AIDS.*

If your heart doesn't go out to the translator who has to render this statement into another language, we need to check to make sure it's still beating. This creatively worded sentence, from a campaign for the ultra-hip MAC Cosmetics brand, is full of translation challenges. Not only must the translator reckon with the compound word *lavender-lovely* but also with the *Yes, we can!* slogan popularized by Barack Obama. Oh, and did we mention that the target market consists of 113 million people whose elected leader is not Obama, but Felipe Calderón?

This is the kind of prose that Eleonora Cisneros González, a Spanish translator based in Mexico, translates for MAC all the time. MAC is well known for the training that it provides to its makeup artists all around the world, and even though she isn't a makeup artist herself, Cisneros González knows this material in great depth. She translates all the material for basic training for makeup artists and the continual stream of training updates on all new collections and products. She also translates the company's manual for its makeup artists.[14]

But the inspirations behind the collections present some of the most complicated challenges for the translator. As in the example given at the start of this section, creative writers of the English text include frequent references to people or concepts that are popular only in America. Another challenge is that they often play with words in such a way that the product names rhyme, create puns, or even seem poetic. Sometimes they use slang, or even invent new words for product names.

Translating for the cosmetic industry also requires a lot of research. You'll not only find dictionaries and glossaries in Cisneros González's library but bilingual makeup books too. Internet research is critical, because it's more current and likely to have information on new trends. Web pages and blogs for which professional makeup artists and fans write and share their knowledge are important sources of information that can help her come up with the best translation. In addition, she also goes into the shops to look at products and read labels to stay current. "Whenever I have a magazine in my hands, I never put it down without reading the makeup section, because it's very relevant for my job," she says. She has also compiled her own glossary based on the many years she has worked for MAC.

Looking at magazines as part of your work? Trying on cosmetics in department stores in the name of research? This kind of translation helps companies like MAC sell their products in other markets. And, it just goes to show that there is a job out there for every young girl (or boy) who loves playing with makeup, so long as she (or he) also loves to play with words. And, in case you're wondering how to say *a lavender-lovely Fergie* in Spanish, Cisneros González conveyed this as "*una Fergie encantadoramente envuelta en colores lavanda.*" (The back-translation? "A Fergie charmingly wrapped in lavender hues.")

Global Glamour

How does an Italian fashion brand know if its new product line is being received well in an English-speaking market like the United States? The marketing team can get a sense of the buzz it's creating when it receives a review titled "Rough and Ready: Take the Rough with the Smooth with Miu Miu's Texture Heels." *But* what if the review is in English, and not all of the Italian-speaking marketing staff who need to read it can understand that language? That's where translator Sara Radaelli comes in. She converts the review from English into Italian on behalf of Miu Miu, one of the many high-end fashion houses whose international press clippings she translates. She performs translations of articles like these so that the public relations and marketing staff can understand exactly how the product is being received by the fashion press in local markets. She diligently annotates her translation, making sure that the client understands that "taking the rough with the smooth" in English plays on the idea of contrast.

Very few translators speak the language of luxury. And, even though Radaelli translates from French and English into Italian, it's her ability to navigate the preferred terminology of high-end customers that differentiates her work. A native of Milan, she translates such content not only for Miu Miu, but for Prada, Louis Vuitton, Cartier, Rolex, Miu Miu, Omega, Dior, Hermès, Harry Winston, Dolce & Gabbana, Emilio Pucci, and LaCoste.[15]

Radaelli finds some of the most challenging terminology in articles from the media, which are often riddled with slang terms. Sometimes, cultural references can be problematic, but so too can references to different types of clothing or fabric. She points out that many terms from the fashion world are not translated into Italian, but often stay in English or French. For example, the word for skirt suit in Italian is the French word *tailleur*. Likewise, French words such as *culottes* or *bustier* stay in French when translated into English because they have become part of the language.

Working for luxury brands is not always glamorous. Much of the translation work is dry—such as boilerplate text for legal contracts and repetitive material in catalogs. But all in all, it is important work. Translators who work in this area are not just translating words for their clients. They are helping them build their global images.

Multilingual Is the New Black

Speaking of the importance of image, there's one group of translators that have their fingers on the pulse of emerging trends. Style guru Tim Gunn raves about their work. Popular fashion brands such as Coach, Juicy Couture, and Michael Kors rely on them too. So do the brands that you see on display every day at your local shopping mall, like Oakley, Fossil, Estée Lauder, and Reebok. You'll find their influence at your local Target, Kohl's, and Macy's and in catalogs like Land's End and Victoria's Secret. Those trends you see appearing in the mainstream this month? They knew about these fads more than a year ago. You might even say that they fuel the fashion industry.

"They" are the translators who work at Stylesight, a trend forecasting company that provides coverage not just of fashion, but of style and design for clothing, accessories, and interiors. The company reviews trends and creates forecasts not just based on what they see on the runway, but by what they find happening in local markets. Trends travel the globe, and these translators enable that information to be harvested and understood locally.

Stylesight views its trend reporting service as "global connective knowledge" that is produced by hundreds of editors and correspondents working all over the world. These individuals generate trend images and content every minute of each day. To share the information with its clients across the globe, the company translates it into five languages.

The information created by the Stylesight network includes not only its website but newsletters that go out daily, weekly, and monthly. And perhaps surprising, one of the biggest areas of content that requires translation is its image library, which contains nearly eight million images. Why do images need translation? Well, remember, a picture is worth a thousand words. Each image is tagged with keywords—maybe not a thousand of them, but certainly enough to help visitors easily find them and understand the details of what is conveyed within a given picture.

Keyword translation might sound simple, but it's actually quite complex. Sometimes, a single word can be more difficult to translate because it doesn't benefit from the context of the rest of a sentence. Each keyword has to be defined carefully, taking into account its relationship with other cultures and languages. Think about how you would try to explain terms like *grunge* or *utility chic* to a ninety-year-old, and you'll get the idea. Converting phrases such as *bomber-cape hybrid, plasticized lace, quilted calico,* and *peekaboo tulle* into another language can be a daunting task, but it keeps the fashion industry churning.

Stylesight's translation department is based in New York, where they have in-house talent for Chinese, Japanese, Korean, Spanish, and Turkish. The team consists not only of translation managers and language editors but graphic designers who speak multiple languages. Again, where image matters, images matter. The designers not only have to lay out text in other languages but pick fonts that will work for those languages, add line breaks, and so on.

"This is not a service that any external translation agency would be able to provide," explains Francis Wong, senior vice president and creative director at Stylesight. "It requires a deep understanding of the knowledge our team has built over many years."[16] The translation team interacts constantly with the original writers and creative directors, even providing feedback and ideas that end up being incorporated into the original reports before publication.

Not every term gets translated. Sometimes, a given descriptor is left in-language, or in some cases, a bit more explanation is required. "Often, after translation, a sentence can get much longer or much shorter," Wong points out. "Spanish is often double the length when compared to the same sentence in Chinese." With such meaning-packed terms as *mannish minimalism, scuba-inspired jeggings, raffia-embellished pinafores,* and *underwear as outerwear,* it's no wonder Stylesight requires professional translators to make sense of them and convert them into other languages.

Pay for Translation Now or Laser Removal Later

Opinions on the aesthetic value of tattoos can go either way, but experience teaches us there's a really good chance that foreign-language tattoos will end only in embarrassment. Just ask Rihanna, the pop star with *rebelle fleur* inked into her neck. If she had really wanted a "rebel flower" tattoo, it might have been wise to first consult a professional French translator, who would have suggested its correct form: *fleur rebelle*. Still, the two languages that Americans most often botch with their tattoos must be Hebrew and Chinese. In fact, there's a blog for each language (http://hanzismatter. blogspot.com and www.badhebrew.com) devoted exclusively to the linguistic follies of tattoo artists and their clients.

Behind the Scenes with Beauty Queens

Far from the New York fashion scene, the air is thick with the scents of hairspray and fake tanning mist. A mixture of sequins, hair extensions, and false eyelashes speckle the floor. A bevy of young women stand in line, clad in the tiniest of bikinis to accentuate their bodies, about a third of which have been surgically enhanced, to the delight of the nearly six hundred million viewers around the world. You guessed it—it's time for the Miss Universe pageant.

Not surprising for a beauty contest, the Miss Universe competition scores the contestants almost entirely on their looks. A woman's chances of getting into the final round are based primarily on two things: how little she leaves to the imagination in a swimsuit and how well she fills out an evening gown. But there's a third part of the pageant—the interview portion. For this part of the competition, an interpreter can make or break a contestant's dreams.

Latin America is famous for repeated successes on the global pageant stage. Six out of the last ten winners hailed from Spanish-speaking countries such as Mexico, Panama, Puerto Rico, Venezuela, and the Dominican Republic. When a contestant does not speak English fluently, she relies on an interpreter to communicate critical details about her personality that can sway the outcome of the contest. In an interview, the judges sit on the edges of their seats, waiting to learn the contestants' answers. For situations like these, interpreters are essential. In fact, in the 2011 pageant, some commentators felt that Miss Philippines, who answered in English, did not have the same advantage as the non-English-speaking finalists, because she did not benefit from the additional time to process and think through the question (this presumes that the contestants have some basic level of English comprehension, but require the interpreter to ensure they fully understand what is said).

But interpreters help the beauty contestants far beyond just the interactions that take place on camera. They accompany the non-English-speaking Misses for weeks on end as they engage in other pageant activities and rehearse for the live telecast. From stage directions to walking them through the different sections of the program, interpreters help the women communicate with everyone from the camera crew to the choreographers. Sometimes they even do voice-over work for the segments that introduce each contestant to viewers.

Interpreters are most visible when a contestant reaches the final round and has to answer an interview question on camera. These circumstances present special challenges for interpreters. First of all, the interpreter has no idea what the questions will be, let alone

how the contestant will respond. Add to that the fact that the interpreter may not even be able to hear what she needs to interpret. "It's
difficult to hear properly when you're on a big stage and everybody's
nervous," explains María Cristina de la Vega, who has interpreted
for ten Miss Universe pageants throughout her career.[17]

But even when the interpreter can hear properly, there are other
challenges. For example, interpreters typically don't take notes
while on camera for pageants because it can be distracting to the
audience. But when contestants get nervous, they often ramble
on and on without pausing to allow the interpreter to provide their
answer in English. De la Vega recalls interpreting for a young lady
who was asked on-camera who her favorite poet was. "She launched
into a fast, incoherent, and long-winded rendering of a folk poem
from her childhood as I stared at her in dismay," she recalls. Meanwhile, the audience looked on with interest wondering what she was
saying. "Knowing that it was next to impossible to give a verbatim
interpretation, I turned to the camera and in a calm and measured
tone, interpreted the stanzas I had retained and then gave a gist of
the whole."

As the saying goes, "the show must go on." In the case of international beauty pageants, interpreters enable that to happen.

Whetting (and Wetting) Your Appetite

Plenty of companies get international brand names wrong. And
when we say wrong, we mean so wrong that their product name
becomes a laughingstock. This is especially true when it comes to
food items.

If you don't believe us, allow us to offer you a nice glass of Fart, a frosted mug of Fat, or a refreshing sip of Pee Cola to prove our point. Contrary to what you might think, these are not beverages invented by five-year-olds. They're actual product names for a juice drink in Poland (Fart), a beer in Sweden (Fat), and a soft drink in Ghana (Pee Cola).

There are certain foreign products that cause even the most stoic among us to break a smile. Other examples of beverages that just "don't translate well" for the English-speaking market include the likes of Erektus (a Czech sports drink), Dickmilch (a German yogurt drink), Bra (a Swedish yogurt), and Baldanis (a French liqueur).

Feeling hungry? It isn't just drinks that are poorly named for global marketing. Equally cringe-worthy names have been given to plenty of other items, such as Bimbo (Mexican sandwich bread), JussiPussi (Finnish dinner rolls), Prick (Brazilian potato chips), and Only Puke (a Chinese snack food). If these foods are too bland, you can always add flavor to your meal with a packet of Çemen (a Turkish sauce) or a can of Shitto (a spicy pepper sauce from Ghana).

If you still have room for dessert, you can indulge in some chocolate candy, such as Asse (Japanese), Big Nuts (Belgian), Crap's (French), Creamy Ball (Japanese), or Plopp (Czech). And in case you'd like to stick with English-language products, if you're an American, you can always open up a can of spotted dick (a British dessert). Or, if you're British, you can eat some Fannie Mae Candies ("fanny" is an innocent enough word in American English, but for the British, it's a vulgar word for female genitalia).

Yes, these are all actual product names from different countries around the world. Granted, many of them changed their names long ago, after realizing that the names looked funny to foreigners, but others (like Bimbo bread and spotted dick) are popular enough in their home countries that there is no sign of them changing any-time soon.

On the other hand, if you have a friend or relative who is fond of forwarding "interesting" email messages to you, chances are that you've heard about some other food product names that, when translated into other languages, didn't do so well. For example, per-haps you've heard the one about Coca-Cola supposedly translating its name into Chinese as "bite the wax tadpole"? Here's the truth behind that tale. In 1928, when Coca-Cola first started selling its products in China, the company had not actually selected the sym-bols to represent its name yet. However, shopkeepers began creating signs to emulate the sounds of the product. Some of these characters resulted in some nonsensical meanings, and "bite the wax tadpole" was reportedly one of the many combinations that resulted.

But the characters that Coca-Cola ultimately registered for its Chinese trademark in 1928 represented a rather pleasant concept, something along the lines of "allowing the mouth to rejoice." No matter how good it may taste, there is certainly much to be said for choosing a product name wisely, so that it works not only in the local market, but in translation. At the very least, a good translation can prevent consumers from putting an item back on the shelf be-fore they even give it a try.

Shopping Tips

Here is a helpful hint to remember when reading labels in a foreign grocery store. *Preservative* (English), *préservatif* (French), *Präservativ* (German), *prezervativ* (Romanian, Czech, Croatian), *preservativ* (Slo-venian), *preservativo* (Italian, Spanish, Portuguese), *prezerwatywa*

(Polish), презерватив (Russian, Serbian, Bulgarian), *prezervatif* (Turkish), *præservativ* (Danish), *prezervatyvas* (Lithuanian), *Prezervatīvs* (Latvian), and *preservatiu* (Catalan) all sound alike and are actually all derived from the same Latin word. And they all mean the same thing. All but one. Only the English word does not mean "condom."

Come Dine with Me

Imagine inviting someone to lunch. Which term for *lunch* would you choose? The answer might seem fairly straightforward in English, but it isn't always so simple for some languages. What if you had to issue your invitation in Spanish? The three meals of the day that you'll typically learn in a basic Spanish class are *desayuno* (breakfast), *almuerzo* (lunch), and *cena* (dinner). Easy, right? Not so fast—out of these three, the only mealtime term that you can safely use almost anywhere in the Spanish-speaking world without any risk of being misunderstood is *desayuno*. That means the first meal of the day in most of the Spanish-speaking world.

It's after breakfast that things start to get tricky. In Colombia, you might be served a meal after breakfast called *mediasnueves* or *mediamañana*. However, go to some parts of Mexico, especially rural areas, and around that time of day you'll be served *almuerzo* instead. *Almuerzo* isn't lunch in this case, but something more like brunch, because it falls between breakfast and lunch.

Of course, in many places where Spanish is spoken, *almuerzo* means lunch instead of brunch—but not everywhere. In Spain and in many parts of Mexico, lunch is called *la comida* instead. But head over to Cuba, Puerto Rico, Colombia, and Peru, and *la comida* means supper, not lunch. To confuse matters even further, *la comida* is also the word for food in general. We're not kidding!

Even though Ecuador borders both Peru and Colombia, supper isn't called *la comida* there, but rather *la merienda*. In nearly every other country, a *merienda* is a snack. If you want to talk about dinner in most Spanish-speaking places, you could always use *la cena* instead. Several countries, like Mexico, Panama, Argentina, Spain, Costa Rica, and Venezuela, use *la cena* for the third main meal of the day. *Cena* is understood in other places, too, but often implies a more formal meal (think dinner instead of supper).

Terminological differences can be fun and interesting for sure, but professional translators have to know a lot more than just "how to speak Spanish" to do their job well. Often, knowing just one Spanish is not enough.

Authentic American Cuisine

You might think of beef jerky as something typically American, but the word actually comes from *charki*, a word from Quechua, the language of the Incas, which is still spoken in Peru and Ecuador today. What could be more American than grilling in the summertime? Well, the word *barbecue* also comes from an indigenous language–an Arawakan language of Haiti, from which *barbakoa*, meaning "framework of sticks," was taken. And what about pecan pie? The word *pecan* comes from the Illinois word *pakani*. Squash comes from the Narragansett word *askútasquash*. Several words also made their way into English from Nahuatl, such as avocado (*āhuacatl*), cocoa (*cacahuatl*), and chili (*chīlli*).

Mi Café Es Su Café

Translators aren't the only ones who have to wrestle with the reality of "universal Spanish," the name often given to Spanish spoken by the diverse immigrant groups that make up the Spanish-speaking population in the United States (though the term implies even broader use). Companies spend a lot of time and money fine-tuning their marketing messages to get them just right for this demographic. For example, the Nestlé company, which sells its products in eighty-six countries around the world, is what you might call an old pro at marketing across cultures. Its worldwide brand recognition is due in part to the significant attention it pays to language issues, something that dates back to its very roots.

Back in the 1830s, the company's founder, Heinrich Nestle, changed his own name to Henri Nestlé in order to make it more French-sounding. Heinrich was originally from Frankfurt but felt that an adapted version of his name would make it more suitable for Vevey, the French-speaking region of Switzerland where he started the company, and where it remains headquartered today. So, in many senses, the Nestlé name itself is a translation.

Fast-forward to the present. Nestlé is a popular brand in many countries, but especially in Latin America, where it has operated for nearly a hundred years. "One of the surprising things we've encountered in focus groups with consumers from Latin America is how strongly they believe that Nestlé is a company from their country of origin," explains Juan Motta, head of emerging markets domestic. "When we state that Nestlé is a global company based in Switzerland, they don't believe it, since it's a brand they grew up with."[18] It makes sense. When you think of Nestlé-owned brands like Juicy

Juice, Hot Pockets, and Lean Cuisine, do you envision a chalet at the foot of the Swiss Alps? Chances are that an American household jumps to mind instead.

The company also applies its multicultural expertise within the U.S. market. Motta's division focuses on two main groups: Hispanic and Asian consumers living within the United States. The company takes Nestlé brands that are already popular in the home markets of foreign-born U.S. consumers and brings them into the American market, sometimes with adaptations to reflect a new life abroad.

One example of how this process works is Nestlé's development of a new product for the U.S. Hispanic market based on Nescafé Clásico, a coffee product that was successful in Latin America. Because Latin American coffee drinkers often earn more money when they settle in the United States, the types of products they want to buy also evolve. Their palates may change along with how they view a food item. That's why words cannot merely be taken out of one language and dropped into another. "Coffee in the USA is not the same thing as *café* in Latin America," Motta explains. "The connotations of U.S. mainstream coffee are more functional and focused on caffeine to start your day, whereas in Latin America they are more emotional and related to social interaction." To reflect the position of U.S. Hispanics straddling both worlds, Nestlé introduced a product called Nescafé Clásico Suave, which uses a smoother roast and caters to a milder palate than the original Nescafé Clásico.

In fact, the company recently launched a bilingual and bicultural website, www.elmejornido.com (*el mejor nido* means "the best nest.") The site displays products like Abuelita Almond and La Lechera Condensed Milk. At Thanksgiving, you'll see a recipe not for the traditional American pumpkin pie, but for pumpkin flan instead. Visitors can easily toggle between English and Spanish, making the approach more targeted to the linguistic reality of the U.S. Hispanic market.

Is there anything about Nestlé that does not get adapted? In its original German, the *Nestle* surname (without the accent) meant "little nest." Throughout the globe, the corporate logo displays a little nest with three birds, which represent Heinrich (later known as Henri) and his two brothers. That stays consistent, no matter what. While products and their names can often be translated and adapted for new markets, brands often remain stable, even when crossing borders.

Bordeaux Without Borders

Translation affects all kinds of tastes. Consider the following:

> *Pale gold in color, this wine smells of white flowers and lemon curd, with a hint of sweet oak. It offers an explosion of crushed wet rocks in the mouth. The tender and beautifully filigreed flavors of tart unripe apples and lemon curd vie for attention. Beautifully bright acidity zips the wine along the palate, leaving a waxy parchment quality in the lingering finish.*

So reads a typical description of a newly launched wine. For those who are not connoisseurs of wine, it might as well be written in a foreign language.

Few and far between are the people whose taste buds are so

finely tuned to the breadth of wine flavors that they can write about it with such detail and flair, even in their native language. Likewise, there are only a select number of translators in the world who specialize in rendering wine-related content into other languages. This work requires fluency in two tongues, but one could argue that the wine-focused translator also needs a third tongue, one that is highly sensitive to the spectrum of tastes that exist among reds, whites, rosés, and sparkling wines.

Why, you may ask, does the wine industry need translation? The demand for translated wine-related information spans a greater number of areas than you might realize. Think beyond the bottle itself and its labeling, which requires translation of the ingredients for export into most countries. Consider all the legal aspects, such as patents for winemaking equipment, technical standards for winemaking from dozens of countries, legislation and trade disputes, and geographical indications. And there are the business documents—harvest production reports, partnership agreements with distributors, and export/import documentation.

Then comes advertising, from magazine ads to commercials and online videos that are launched by wineries from other countries. There are also websites for wineries with content that must be translated. For example, Ernest & Julio Gallo's online property is available in seven languages—Chinese, English, French, German, Japanese, Korean, and Spanish. Once a wine is launched, the tasting notes from award-winning sommeliers and reviews in leading fine wine publications also need to be translated in order for the winery to gauge the success of the wine, and to repurpose those reviews for additional advertising and marketing opportunities.

Kirk Anderson translates all of these types of texts, but the tasting notes are his favorite type of project because they allow him to use the skills and knowledge he has accumulated over the course of nearly two decades.[19] The care that he takes with selecting his words reflects the attention with which he chooses a wine. Kirk, a trained sommelier, is the first to admit that tasting notes often sound like nonsense to the nonenthusiast. However, he emphasizes that the accurate translation of flavors, aromas, and colors used to describe the wine is critical. This detail provides readers with important insight into the techniques, region, process, and aging used to bring the wine from the vineyard to the glass.

"Calling a Chardonnay *buttery* may sound patently absurd to some, but it's a clear sign that the wine has undergone malolactic fermentation, transforming the malic acid, that often offers a hint of the aroma and bite of a Granny Smith apple, into lactic acid, common in dairy products," Kirk explains. He adds, "Nuanced colors in a wine indicate aging, so you can be pretty confident that a more opaque red wine is younger than one that 'fades to garnet at the rim.'" As a professional translator, he takes his subject matter seriously.

While the flavor-related terms can border on the poetic, making them both fun and challenging to translate, Kirk has noticed a new trend in his wine-focused translation work. Increasingly, wine descriptions are focusing more on the vineyard itself. "Arguably, the best wines are grown, not produced in the winery, so being able to write intelligently about wine-growing techniques is rapidly becoming essential for translators in this field." In addition to knowing how to say things like *biscuity*, *plummy*, and *fleshy* without making them sound ridiculous in another language, translators like Kirk also need knowledge in agricultural terminology that includes

soil types, trellising techniques, and grafting. Indeed, wine translation has an expansive scope that spans everything from the field to
the table.

So keep this in mind the next time you raise your next glass of
imported wine: from the label on the bottle down to the machine
used to plow the fields where the grapes were grown, every last drop
reaches your lips thanks to translation.

Some Things Just Sound Better in French

"To start, I suggest something blown by the wind, followed by fat
liver and a dainty thick slice. And how about some burned cream for
dessert?" Chances are, if your waiter greeted you with these words,
you'd get up and leave the restaurant. But just substitute these
phrases for their equivalent terms in French—*vol-au-vent*, *foie gras*,
filet mignon, and *crème brûlée*—and suddenly you've got your appetite back. Translation? No, thanks!

We'll Drink to That

"Cheers!" It's a term uttered by English speakers after many a toast
at international gatherings, and it's been featured in many an ad
campaign for alcoholic beverages, but it's one of those words that
presents a special challenge in translation. The word or phrase that
people say before having a drink differs greatly from one place to
another. The translation of the word *cheers* provides a perfect example of how many terms—especially ones that are deeply rooted
in culture—cannot be translated literally.

The word *cheers* as a predrink salutation came into English from the word *chere*, which was used in medieval times to mean expression or mood. By 1919, the word as most English speakers know and use it today became popular in Britain. Essentially, the person uttering the word *cheers* is wishing others a good time and an enjoyable drink. So how do you create the same effect in other languages?

In Danish, Norwegian, and Swedish, you'll say *skål*, which is similar to *skál* in Faroese and Icelandic. Urban legend has it that the reason this word is used for *cheers* is that the Vikings used to drink out of their enemies' skulls. Actually, the word does not have any linguistic link to the word *skull*; it means "bowl" or "drink vessel." Instead of using skulls (messy!), Norsemen preferred to drink out of a cow's horn, because they were easier to obtain and naturally hollow.

In a wide array of languages throughout the world, the word *cheers* essentially translates into wishing someone good health. This is the case for languages like Spanish (*salud*), Italian (*salute*), French (*à votre santé*), Irish (*sláinte*), Russian (на здоровье), and Bulgarian (наздраве). In German, it's typical to wish someone good health when drinking wine (*zum Wohl*). However, beer calls for a different sentiment (*prost*, which comes from the Latin *prosit*, meaning "may it be good").

For many languages, it's more customary to wish someone a long life, such as Hebrew (לְחַיִּים), Armenian (կենացդ), Turkish (*şerefe*), and Serbian (живели). In others, no well-wishing is needed—instead, a simple "bottoms up" will suffice. Languages like Japanese (乾杯), Chinese (干杯), and Korean (건배) instruct people to "dry the glass." And in Bengali, it's customary to wish them victory (জয়).

So, at your next opportunity to attend a gathering where people speak multiple languages, if you want to be extra careful to minimize the risk of mistranslation and make sure you're understood across most languages and cultures, we suggest saying something like the following, "I wish you a long and victorious life, full of health and good luck. Now, bottoms up, and have a great time!"

Internationalize Those Fries

A cup of sodden rice with chicken, ginger, onion, shallots, and chili peppers. A fried patty made of potatoes, peas, and spices, topped with tomatoes and vegetarian mayonnaise. Grilled chicken in pita bread with lettuce, tomato, onion, and tahini sauce. English muffins topped with refried beans, white cheese, and salsa. Breaded chicken covered in guacamole. A deep-fried roll of beef ragout. Lamb wrapped in Arabic flat-bread with shredded lettuce and tomatoes. A sandwich made of grilled salmon and dill sauce.

Do any of these dishes sound like they could possibly come from the same restaurant? While it might seem unlikely, they actually do. It's the same restaurant chain with locations in different countries. Let's try referring to these menu items as you would order them locally: Bubur Ayam McD (Malaysia), McAloo Tikki (India), McArabia (Egypt), McMollete (Mexico), McPollo (Chile), McKroket (Netherlands), McTurco (Turkey), and McLaks (Norway).

Yes, to the delight of many Americans and to the dismay of many others, the golden arches of McDonald's appear throughout the world. But the menu items vary greatly. Go to a McDonald's in Singapore, and you can order jasmine tea and a Shaka Shaka Chicken, which you create by dumping spice powder into a bag and, with a quick "shaka" of the bag, coating your chicken patty in local spices. In Spain, you can actually buy the country's chilled soup, gazpacho, at McDonald's, where it is served in a carton. In Brazil, you'll find McDonald's filling that rectangular apple pie crust with bananas instead.

The burgers that made McDonald's famous also vary tremendously by country. Head to Japan and you can order a Koroke Burger, which consists of mashed potato, cabbage, and katsu sauce. In Hong Kong, you'll find a burger that is served not between sesame seed buns, but between rice cakes. In Malaysia, you can order a Double Beef Prosperity Burger, which features spicy black pepper sauce. In Italy, the burgers come with pancetta and usually are on ciabatta rolls. Visit India, where eating beef is against religious rules for about 80 percent of the population, and you won't find any beef burgers on the menu whatsoever.

In Germany, you can pick up a McSausage Burger. In Greece, a Greek Mac. In New Zealand, a KiwiBurger. In Costa Rica, a McPinto Deluxe, with rice, beans, and plantains. In Thailand, a McSamurai Pork Burger. Head to the United Kingdom around Christmastime, and you can order a mincemeat and custard pie for dessert. When in France, you can order Le McWrap Chèvre, a goat cheese wrap. In Argentina, you can have wine with your McDonald's meal; German outlets of McDonald's sell beer; in Israel, kosher food is served; and in Hawaii, you'll be handed Spam with your breakfast. How's that for contrast?

McDonald's is a global company, but it makes most of its money in just a few countries. About 70 percent of its revenue, which normally tops $20 billion annually, comes from restaurants in Australia, Canada, China, France, Germany, Japan, the United Kingdom, and of course, the United States. While some of its products, such as its fries (in France, they're called *pommes frites* (fried potatoes) instead of French fries), stay consistent at most of its global locations, the brand is well known for adapting its menu for other countries. Here's the question: If the company introduces new products in different countries to cater to local tastes and sticks with old favorites like fries and soft-serve ice cream whenever possible, what does translation have to do with its success?

Two words: human resources. In 2011, there were 1.7 million people employed by McDonald's restaurants. With thirty-three thousand restaurants in 119 countries, those employees obviously speak a lot of different languages. Aside from management, fast-food employees are typically not looking for lifetime employment or even full-time work. They might only work at the restaurant for a summer, or a year, or on weekends. Yet they have to follow the same processes each time to prepare the food the same way. They need to operate the equipment safely, being mindful of on-the-job safety hazards. All this information has to be communicated to them somehow.

All over the world, there are translators who localize and translate the training software that McDonald's uses to train its employees. From making a green tea McFlurry in Japan to serving customers at a "ski-through" location in Sweden, all of these employees need to be trained in their native language to ensure that they understand how to prepare the food safely and according to company specifications. And before that can happen, their training materials have to be translated. So yes, translators contribute to McDonald's success, far more than you might have suspected. Just don't blame us for the world's expanding waistline.

Green Dots for Meat Shunners

Comedian Andy Rooney once joked that the original meaning of the word *vegetarian* was "lousy hunter," but in Ireland, a little more choice is implied. The Irish Gaelic word for *vegetarian* is *feoilséantóir*, which translates literally as "meat shunner." In India, where more than 30 percent of the population observe a vegetarian diet, all packaged foods are labeled with either a green dot (signifying vegetarian-friendly) or a red dot (not vegetarian-friendly), making words even less necessary.

CHAPTER 6

Entertaining Fans and Playing to the Crowd in Translation

A different language is a different vision of life.

—Federico Fellini,
Italian film director

And the Oscar for Best Interpreter Goes to . . .

When Jack Jason was a baby, his parents did not sing him lullabies. They didn't listen for his cries on a baby monitor, or comment on the sweet sound of their newborn son's coos. When he spoke his first words, they didn't hear them. Yet Jason's parents were some of the most loving, supportive, and attentive parents that one could imagine. They just happened to be Deaf.

Jack Jason is known as a CODA, a child of deaf adults. As with most CODAs born in the United States, American Sign Language (ASL)—not English—is his native language. He grew up in California, so the only voice in his house was the voice on television. As he got older, Jason eventually became part of the hearing world, went to school, and learned to speak English (and Spanish).

Contrary to popular belief, sign language is not universal—there are hundreds of signed languages in use throughout the world. For example, there are more than eighteen different sign languages used in Spanish-speaking countries. Wherever there are large communities of people who are deaf, signed languages emerge naturally, and usually without any dependence on spoken languages. Linguists have proven that signed languages are every bit as rich and complex as spoken languages. In fact, sign language tends to be more efficient than spoken language. For example, to tell a story in English takes 4.7 words per second, compared with 2.3 signs per second for ASL. These stats come from a psycholinguist and cognitive neuroscientist by the name of Ursula Bellugi. She studied people fluent in both ASL and English, and found that these individuals needed 210 words to tell a story in English, but could tell the same story in ASL with only 122 signs.[1]

Another misconception is that sign language is all in the hands. In actuality, it is far more complex than that, which is why pictures of hand positions are insufficient to communicate in sign language. For example, in ASL, the same sign may mean something completely different depending on where it is in reference to the signer's body. The direction of the hand and where it is pointed is important for the meaning of the word. Facial expressions are also critical and can dramatically affect the meaning.

As a child, Jason not only crossed language barriers—he served as the bridge between two completely different cultures—the Deaf and the hearing worlds. The term *Deaf* is capitalized to denote people who are typically deaf since birth or a very young age and who identify themselves as culturally deaf in addition to physically deaf. When his teachers complained that Jason was getting in trouble for talking too much at school, his parents were delighted. They were glad their son was getting along so well in the hearing world. Of course, Jason was also the one interpreting for those parent–teacher meetings. In fact, Jason interpreted for all kinds of situations—everything from driving directions to interpreting for his mom at a Mary Kay cosmetics party. Even as a child, he felt proud of his ability to navigate two languages so smoothly and help his parents communicate with the hearing community. Interpreting always felt easy for him.[2]

Fast-forward to today, and you'll see Jason in some situations that also have a lot riding on them, but he's as relaxed and at ease interpreting as he was as a kid. One moment you'll find him rendering an acceptance speech at the Academy Awards. The next, you'll see him standing next to Hollywood stars at galas and charity events. Turn on the television, and there he is, speaking to Larry King, Ellen, or Donald Trump. Peer over at the White House lawn, and you'll find him having a conversation with President Obama. Jason interprets professionally for only one person, but she happens to be the most famous Deaf person in the world—Marlee Matlin.

An Oscar-winning actress, Matlin has a lot riding on her interpreter's skills. While Matlin's career success is due to her skill as an actress and her willingness to push boundaries, the ability to showcase her unique personality to the hearing world depends in great part on his work. That's probably why, in her bestselling autobiography, *I'll Scream Later,* Jason is one of the first people she thanks in the acknowledgments.[3]

But Matlin does more than just express her appreciation for Jason in her book. He appears throughout the book, which chronicles her life and career, in numerous anecdotes and photos. She writes extensively about how they first met, how he became her only friend in New York when her career was just starting out, and how today, he runs her production company and works with her as a creative partner. Perhaps the most remarkable words Matlin writes about Jason have to do with his ability to interpret.

"The memory that stays with me the most is how well he signed," she recalls. "He was so fast I had to ask him if he was Deaf. I'd never seen a hearing person who could sign like that." Matlin goes on to explain how Jason suggested once, when she was first getting to know him, that they go see a movie. When she reminded him that she wouldn't be able to read lips on screen and that there was no captioning, he did not see a problem—instead, he volunteered to interpret the entire two-hour movie. Most working sign language interpreters need to take a break after every half hour. Not Jack Jason. And so off they went to see the *Color Purple*. Matlin comments, "During the film, I was amazed and fascinated by Jack's ability, how he was able to deliver the subtext of the movie as well as the dialogue. It was a long movie, and at the end he was crying while interpreting it all for me. I couldn't believe he could do that. I thought to myself that he had to be the best interpreter in the world."

Anyone who has seen Jason interpret on shows like the *Celebrity Apprentice* or *Dancing with the Stars* knows that his delivery into English is equally impressive. His voice is pleasant and confident but can convey a tremendous range of emotion, the perfect auditory mirror of Matlin's expressive face and body language. It's both a joy to watch Matlin and a pleasure to hear Jason. At times, the two seem to be one. After all, Jason is more than an interpreter for Matlin—he's a business partner and a friend. And Jason was there not only for her wedding, but for the births of her four children—the children who saw their mom *sign*—rather than *sing*—their lullabies. Just like Jack Jason's parents did.

> ## Deaf Culture
>
> In some places, Deaf culture is very strong due to hereditary deaf-ness among large portions of the population. In the village of Ben-kala in North Bali, a unique sign language called Kata Kolok has been developed in complete isolation from other sign languages. Local stories even include deaf ghosts and a deaf god.

Linguistic Acrobats

Unlike actors, circus performers such as trapeze artists, stilt-walkers, clowns, and contortionists do not rely much on spoken language for their performances. They don't necessarily need any-one to help them communicate with their audience. So why does Cirque du Soleil have more than twenty interpreters on staff? So that the performers can communicate with their trainers, and with each other. The interpreting team at Cirque covers fifteen languages, ranging from Bulgarian and Portuguese to Chinese and Russian.[4]

Irina Kravtsova is one of them, but in addition to interpreting, she prepares the schedules of all Cirque's interpreters to make sure they get to where they're needed at the right time. Most of the inter-preters' work involves helping the performers with their training and preparing for the shows, but they frequently do written transla-tion as well. They translate documents related to work conditions, nutrition, and immigration information, but they also translate daily communications, such as emails.

Cirque is well-known for fostering creativity. Kravtsova recalls how, during one artistic class, the coach had invented her own language, with terms like *cave breath*, *fish flob*, and *body grow*. The interpreters had to consult with each other to figure out how to convey these brand-new concepts, which were being invented right in front of them. In another artistic expression class, the coach was doing an exercise with the performers. Kravtsova found herself interpreting such unusual phrases as, "You are a chicken!" "Now you are a drunken chicken!" "Now you are a drunken chicken in love!"

Another interpreter, Marie-Odile Pinet, has been working as a Chinese interpreter with Cirque for more than thirteen years. Most of the artists with whom Pinet works are young—between the ages of eighteen and twenty-six. She serves not only to mediate between two cultures but helps the new arrivals navigate the culture of Cirque itself. She takes them to meetings that can involve everything from contract negotiations to costume measurements to explaining the tax system. She even takes them to the grocery store to ensure that they understand what they're buying. Her work encompasses that of a medical interpreter, legal interpreter, and escort interpreter all in the span of a single day.

As time goes on, the artists usually learn enough English that they no longer need to rely on an interpreter. Cirque provides them with English classes, but the interpreters also help them practice English, especially words that are important for acrobatic training or words that could have an impact on safety. This ensures that everyone can communicate properly in the event of an emergency, even when it's their job to be clowning around.

Until the Fat Lady Sings in English

The great German composer Richard Wagner once said that opera is a *Gesamtkunstwerk*, "a total work of art." In fact, *opera* is the plural form of *opus*, which is Latin for "work." So, in its truest sense, opera actually refers not just to a single work, but a collection of them. Isn't it ironic, then, that an art form such as opera, which depends so heavily on storytelling, is primarily performed in languages that aren't understood by its audiences? Experienced patrons of the opera know that you follow along by reading the text of the opera in what is known as a *libretto*. Husband-and-wife-team Mark Herman and Ronnie Apter work together to translate these libretti into English for operas written in Italian, Russian, French, German, or Czech.[5]

It's a daunting task according to Apter, a retired professor of literature from Central Michigan University. She describes libretto translation as poetry translation with several major differences: The words must be perfectly fitted to the music, the rhythm of the language and the cadence must be matched to the melody, and the translator must consider the diction level that the particular character would use and the physical limitations of what a singer can actually sing. At the same time, the translation must use modern concepts of translation while reflecting the historical flavor of the original.

Herman and Apter have both studied voice. After translating a libretto literally, they work on the lyrical translation of the libretto by singing it to each other—Herman, the low voices; Apter, the high ones—to find out whether their translations fit with the music. If a stressed syllable does not fall on a note that is stressed, the text usually has to be rewritten. If the number of notes in a certain part does not match the number of syllables of the translation, the translated text has to be reworked or placed elsewhere where a better match might be found.

If you've been to an opera recently, you probably heard it performed in its original language, with supertitles containing a distilled version of the lyrics above the stage or in back of the seat in front of you. Herman and Apter think this practice takes away from the power of the opera itself, even more than when you're watching a movie with subtitles.

Many people think that opera, in order to be authentic, must be performed in its original language, preferably Italian, French, or German. (There are, of course, exceptions, such as Philip Glass's opera *Satyagraha* performed in Sanskrit.) This belief reached absurd levels in the eighteenth century when Georg Friedrich Händel, a German composer, wrote Italian operas for an English-speaking audience in London. Views on the importance of sticking to the original language evolved, and by the nineteenth century, most composers assumed their operas would be translated. Unfortunately, as time went on, "snob appeal" trumped clear communication, and lyric translation fell out of favor. So it was a major victory for Herman and Apter when Ricordi, a famed Italian publisher of operas written by giants such as Verdi and Puccini, commissioned them to translate a number of libretti not just into English for the audience to understand, but into versions in English that could actually be performed.

How do English-speaking singers feel about performing in a language that they actually know? Theoretically, all opera singers are expected to have mastered the languages in which they sing. They often haven't, which can have a detrimental effect on their credibility as they act out their roles. As a result, most singers welcome the chance to sing in a language they understand. They realize that acting is often not the strongest part of their repertoire when so much work has been dedicated to training and maintaining their voices.

With translation efforts like Apter's and Herman's, will opera ever become an art form that is fully translated and accessible to the masses, like literature or film? Probably not, Herman ventures. People have been debating whether to translate operas for three hundred years. The prejudice against translated operas, combined with the poor quality of much of what has been translated so far, might prevent opera from ever being embraced widely by those who do not understand the original languages.

So, if you've ever been to the opera and heard a mezzo soprano singing an aria in Italian or a tenor brilliantly singing a refrain in German, ask yourself how much more beautiful the passionate voices and grandiose music would have been if you could have fully understood the story. Perhaps if it were translated into more lan-

Chinese Mamma Mia!

In 2011, the hit show *Mamma Mia!* made its debut in China, proving for the first time that it was possible to adapt a Western musical for Chinese theater. Forget literal translation—the team even incorporated Shanghainese slang to give the dialogue a local flavor. The cast also performed Mongolian and Tibetan folk dances that did not appear in the original. In fact, the adapted version included the

> Twisting Yangko, a traditional dance from the Chinese countryside
> with movements that imitate the action of planting rice. That's def-
> initely something you won't see on Broadway!

guages, opera would even be embraced by the masses as, to quote
Wagner again, a truly intelligible total work of art.

It's Raining Falafel

In contrast to opera, Hollywood provides entertainment for the
masses. One measure of the success of a blockbuster is how many
ticket sales it generates in other countries. Movie titles are critical
for luring the crowds to the theater. Often, those titles include creative wordplay, double meanings, and other things that just don't
translate very well. So they have to be adapted for other countries.

Just take the film *Cloudy with a Chance of Meatballs*. For the
Israeli market, a decision was made to hold the meatballs. Instead,
its title was changed to the more culturally relevant *Rain of Falafel*
(גשם של פלאפל). Some movie titles, when translated, give away more
details about the plot. For example, Woody Allen's movie *Annie Hall*
was launched in German with the title *Urban Neurotic* (*Der Stadt-
neurotiker*), while in Latin America it became *Two Strange Lovers*
(*Dos extraños amantes*).

The recent comedy *Knocked Up* became *Slightly Pregnant* (*Lig-
eramente embarazada*) in South America, while in Italy the title
went toward the other end of the spectrum, *Very Pregnant* (*Molto
incinta*). In French Canada, the title was the rather straightforward

Surprise Pregnancy (*Grossesse surprise*). Similarly, the movie *American Pie* transformed into *Hot Apple Cake* (*Heißer Apfelkuchen*) in German, while in Mexico it was translated as *Your First Time* (*Tu primera vez*).

How about the movie *Lost in Translation*? Was its title rendered faithfully into other languages? Not exactly. In Brazilian Portuguese the title was *Meetings and Missed Meetings* (*Encontros e Desencontros*), while in European Portuguese it was *Love in a Strange Place* (*O Amor É um Lugar Estranho*), and in Italian, *Love Translated* (*L'amore tradotto*). In Polish and German it turned into *Between Worlds* (*Miedzy slowami* and *Zwischen den Welten*), and in Latin America it became *Lost in Tokyo* (*Perdidos en Tokio*). But these translations pale in comparison with our favorite. In French Can-

George Lucas's Backstroke of the West

Revenge of the Sith was one of the most anxiously awaited installments of the *Star Wars* films. As such, a copy of the movie was soon leaked onto the Internet and quickly released in Shanghai as a bootleg DVD with subtitles in Chinese. For some unknown reason, the producer of the DVD also translated the subtitles back into English instead of using the original text, leading to numerous hilarious mistranslations. The title of the film was rendered as the *Backstroke of the West*. Several times in the film, the phrase *it seems* (好像) was mistakenly translated back into English as "good elephant." The term *Jedi Council* was transformed into "Presbyterian church," and *Jedi* on its own was translated as "hopeless situation." Darth Vader's emotional cry of *Noooooooo* (不要) appeared again in English as "Do not want."

ada, the title was translated as *Unfaithful Translation* (*Traduction infidèle*). Somewhere out there, there's a translator with a great sense of irony, and, we're willing to bet, a knowing chuckle.

Springfield via Helsinki

The well-known theme song plays, and the familiar characters—Homer, Marge, Bart, and Lisa, among others—appear on the screen. The title of the episode flashes: "*Kanuunanruokaa.*" In English, it was called "Homerpalooza," and was translated into Finnish by Sari Luhtanen for the animated TV comedy *The Simpsons*. (She's also the translator behind the Finnish subtitles for *30 Rock*, *Frasier*, and various other sitcoms.)[6]

As the coauthor of a well-known Finnish comic strip (*Maisa & Kaarina*), Luhtanen has plenty of experience in comedy. In fact, perhaps no one in Finland is more qualified to translate *The Simpsons*. Not only did she study drama, scriptwriting, and English philology in school, but she translated some of Groening's earliest work, his *Life in Hell* comic books, into Finnish. She has been translating funny content for more than twenty-five years.

But even for a veteran comedy writer with a talent for comedy like Luhtanen, translating *The Simpsons* isn't easy. As she points out, "When you translate a book, you can replace one joke with another and nobody will be the wiser. On television, the jokes are connected with the visual. There is no escape!" It isn't just the visual elements that make translating *The Simpsons* a challenge. The show is filled with allusions—jokes that refer to other people and places, often ones that require knowledge of American pop culture. That single episode, "Homerpalooza," includes at least forty-four separate allusions.[7] Even the episode's title is an allusion that makes reference to the Lollapalooza tour, giving you an idea of how challenging Sari's job really is.

Here's another example of an allusion from *The Simpsons*, as spoken by the newscaster character Kent Brockman: "Residents are advised to stay inside unless you wear sunscreen or are very, very hairy. Experts recommend a class nine, or Robin Williams, level of hair coverage." The teller of the joke assumes that the audience has certain knowledge of pop culture. In this case, not only is the viewer expected to know who Robin Williams is but they need to know details about what he looks like. Most Finnish viewers would be likely to know who a major film star like Robin Williams is, but they may not necessarily know that he is known for also having a lot of body hair. For this reason, allusions are some of the most difficult items to translate.

When faced with a pop-culture reference, Luhtanen has only a few options—translate the term directly, try to come up with a similar humorous reference in Finnish, or omit it entirely from the translation. If she merely translates an allusion, it might be lost on the viewer unless it has sufficient explanation. But it isn't always possible to provide explanations to help people get the joke. There's limited space available on the screen, and we all know that too much explanation can kill a joke. In spite of these challenges, Luhtanen manages to retain the vast majority of jokes that depend on allusion. For example, in one episode, Homer refers to the American candy M&M's. Luhtanen replaces this with a similar candy that is available in Finland.

Another allusion refers to the NBC TGIF lineup, a popular set of sitcoms in the 1980s with its own play on TGIF, defining it as "thank goodness it's funny" instead of the more widely used "thank goodness it's Friday." Rather than try to explain all this to Finnish viewers, Luhtanen transformed that difficult-to-convey concept into the *Tähtikavalkadin* lineup, which roughly means "stars on parade."

To complicate matters further, the animated show is notoriously full of wordplay. When Sari is faced with the daunting tasks of translating the phone calls that Bart makes to Moe's Tavern, asking to speak with people who have names like Mike Rotch or Hugh Jass, she has to come up with names like Anu Saukko. *Anu* is a woman's name, and *Saukko* is a last name, but when spoken together they sound like the Finnish word for "anus." While Bart would likely approve of Luhtanen's translation, she quips, "And for this I went to university!"

All joking aside, Luhtanen feels that her job is to make sure the Finnish viewers enjoy the show without even realizing that the subtitles are there. She occasionally gets feedback that makes her believe she is succeeding. Recently, one *Simpsons* fan contacted her after he had traveled to the United States. He had been anticipating watching new episodes of the show that had not yet been shown in Finland. To his dismay, he could hardly understand the show, in spite of speaking fluent English, because he did not understand the cultural references without the assistance from the translations. He contacted Luhtanen to let her know that he hadn't realized how critical the subtitles were to his enjoyment of the show until he didn't have them available.

The example of this Finnish fan goes to show that, many times, translation involves transferring much more than just words. Work of the kind that Luhtanen does involves translating humor, culture, and making sure that all of these are synchronized perfectly with the animation that viewers see on the screen.

Schau Mir in Die Augen, Kleines

Talk to any German movie buff about great movie quotes and *"Schau mir in die Augen, Kleines"* (Look into my eyes, baby) will almost certainly appear among the top five. Germans love that über-cool line from the classic American film *Casablanca*. If you're scratching your head in confusion, you're in good company on this side of the Atlantic, for there is no such line in the English version. The beloved quote is how the translator of the first version dubbed into German rendered that equally iconic line, "Here's looking at you, kid." Not what you'd call a direct translation, but it's one that's made cultural history.

A Virtual Creation Story

And the translator said, "Let there be Sheng Long: and there was Sheng Long!" Well, sort of. In the 1991 arcade version of the Japanese video game Street Fighter II, the character Sheng Long was launched into virtual reality because of a translator's misunderstanding. This creation story began when the game's main character, Ryu, exclaimed, "If you cannot overcome the Rising Dragon Punch, you cannot win!" (昇龍拳を破らぬ限り、おまえに勝ち目はない！). Unfortunately, the hapless translator misunderstood the rising dragon (昇龍) reference as the introduction of a new character with the Chinese name of Sheng Long (also: 昇龍). The resulting translation: "You must defeat Sheng Long to stand a chance."

Now, as any passionate gamer could easily recognize—you know who you are, fanboys and fangirls—this is the kind of message that makes your heart beat faster. It's the long-awaited hint that indicates how to reach the next level of the game. But no matter how many bleary-eyed days fans spent searching, Sheng Long was nowhere to be found. Gradually, rumors began circulating from shadowy gamers who claimed that they had long since found and easily defeated Sheng Long, only strengthening the others' resolve. The hunt was far from over.

When the popular magazine *Electronic Gaming Monthly* (*EGM*) upped the ante by giving a detailed description of how to find and defeat Sheng Long in their April 1992 edition, the frenzy reached its climax. In December of the same year, after avid gamers spent months trying to track down the elusive character, the magazine "disclosed" that the instructions for finding Sheng Long had all been an April Fool's gag. The character never existed, so of course could not be found.

It's a funny anecdote, but it does make you wonder how any translator could have made such a mistake. One word: *context*! As most game translators will testify, completely isolated and discombobulated segments of text are the norm rather than the exception. This was especially true during the heyday of arcade games that could not be easily installed on a computer and played along with as they were translated. If you've ever played translated games, you know that these kinds of mistakes still happen today, though possibly in a less dramatic fashion.

In fact, Nora Stevens Heath, who specializes in the translation of Japanese games, says that, even today, she frequently deals with missing context, outrageous space restrictions, and a predefined syntax that worked well for the Japanese original but not for the English translation. And added to those difficulties, her audience is picky, to say the least: "Fanboys and -girls can be brutal in a loud and very public way," she says. Still, she feels passionate about her job, knowing that the gaming community is not limited to kids in shady arcades but cuts across all demographics and gender.[8]

And while there may still be some mistranslations, there are also translation triumphs, such as one in a video game called Animal Crossing: Wild World (おいでよ　どうぶつの森). The translators were truly put to the test with a multilevel Japanese pun: the Japanese word *kabu* can mean "turnip" (蕪) or "stock" (株) as in "stock market." The turnip-selling boar in the game is named *Kaburiba*, which therefore has several possible meanings: "stock/turnip market" (株/蕪売り婆), "stock/turnip-selling old woman" (株/蕪売り場), and "an older woman wearing (the kind of) headgear" (that the character actually wears) (被り婆). It would be no problem to translate one of these meanings, but all three? In a stroke of genius, the translator came up with a "Sow Jones" who was in charge of the "stalk market."

Unlike the mistaken creation of Sheng Long, this is an example of true creation, in the almost mythical sense of the word: "And the translator saw that it was very good!"

All Your Mistranslation Are Belong to Us

An Internet meme is a concept that spreads via the World Wide Web in a manner no one could have predicted. "All your base are belong to us," a strange broken English translation spoken by a character named CATS in a 1991 Japanese video game called Zero Wing. This sentence has the dubious honor of becoming one of the most famous Internet memes to date—so much, in fact, that it's often abbreviated AYBABTU or simply AYB. The garbled translation gained notoriety in email and Internet posts and soon began appearing in unlikely everyday scenes and even on T-shirts. Its original meaning of "CATS has taken all of your bases" (君達の基地は、全て CATSがいただいた) is hard to decipher from the botched translation, but it's a great example of a mistranslation spreading and permeating popular culture to become a veritable phenomenon.

The Pride of China in the NBA

Sports and entertainment inhabit similar spheres, with athletes who are often larger-than-life celebrities. And the interpreters who work for them? Often, they are major sports fans. Take Colin Pine.[9] As a student, Pine was far more interested in basketball than he was in languages. He thought he lacked any language talent. But his college roommate had invited him to visit Taiwan, so Pine asked his parents for a nine-week intensive language course and a ticket to Taiwan as a college graduation present. Pine ended up staying in Taiwan for three years. For the first couple of years he taught English at night and worked in an all-Chinese office during the day. During the third year he enrolled in the National Taiwan University for a formal Chinese language program. In his limited spare time, what did the American sports fanatic do when he was far from home? Play pickup basketball games, of course.

Now, this last activity was probably not the first thing Pine thought to put on his résumé when he returned to the United States. However, it certainly ended up helping with the job he landed a few years later, representing a truly larger-than-life figure, someone who held the hopes of more than one billion people in China. Pine became the interpreter for Yao Ming, the most talked-about and anticipated basketball player entering the NBA in 2002.

In the United States, the seven-foot, six-inch (2.29-meter) basketball phenomenon was a sensation, whose every step and game were followed closely, analyzed, and overanalyzed. But in his home country, he was simply—and overwhelmingly—the "Pride of China." As Pine waited anxiously at the Houston airport to meet his famous client for the first time, he suddenly realized the extent of this responsibility. And it showed. When Yao was later asked what he first thought when he saw Pine, he said that he looked "very young and very nervous."

Interpreters typically do not play a starring role, but especially during the 2002 and 2003 NBA season, when the media and fan attention was most intense, Pine's face was on TV alongside Yao's before and after every game of the Houston Rockets. One fan even created a sign dubbing him the Robin to Yao Ming's Batman.

Pine, who today works for the NBA in Shanghai, looks back on that time of his life as "a dream job, but very exhausting." What Pine did for Yao (and Yao's parents, who lived with Yao in Houston) was to intensively decode a new culture and a new life. Aside from his regular interpreting duties, Pine was Yao's driver and driving instructor. He helped him open a bank account and showed his family where to shop in Houston. He even moved in with Yao and his family.

It is interesting that Pine never had to interpret during actual games. Even though he was heavily involved in interpreting as the coaches set up plays and strategy during practice, during the game, the players' physical memory counts most. How much did he have to interpret of the infamous NBA trash talk between players? Not at all, because Pine figured that it was actually to Yao's advantage to miss that element of what was transpiring on the court.

Some of the more public insults—such as those from rival center Shaquille O'Neal—he did interpret to Yao, who handled the jabs with diplomacy and maturity. In fact, looking back on those years, Pine claims that Yao was by far the more mature of the two. Yao, who had lived under intense public scrutiny back home in China since the age of fourteen, seemed to take the inevitable criticism and injury-related setbacks more nonchalantly than his interpreter. "How can you not feel defensive for such a nice person?" Pine asks.

The feature film *The Year of Yao* chronicles Yao's and Pine's first year in the NBA, making clear that the professional relationship between interpreter and employer had developed into a veritable friendship. After Yao's second year in the NBA, Pine was surprised to be asked back for a third year. Yao's improved English skills made the need for interpretation rare, but again, this was a different kind of relationship. In fact, when Yao was asked during an interview around Thanksgiving what he was most thankful for, he said, "My interpreter, Colin."

Take Me Out to the Ball Game

Many young American boys dream of growing up to be baseball stars. Eleven-year-old Kenji Nimura brought those aspirations with him when he moved to Los Angeles from Japan. Nimura's dream was specific. He wouldn't play for just any team. It had to be with *his* team. The Los Angeles Dodgers.[10]

Unfortunately for most aspiring athletes, reality eventually reorders those visions of sporting greatness. And though he played his heart out at his mostly Latino school in West Los Angeles, Nimura, too, finally realized that he wasn't even close to being good enough to play baseball professionally. But it took a bit longer to recognize that during those many years on and around the ballpark, he had picked up a skill that would one day make it possible to live that dream. What was this skill? His fluency in three languages: Japanese, Spanish, and English. Nimura was first hired as the interpreter for the Dodgers' Japanese superstar pitcher Hiroki Kuroda, but his unique combination of languages quickly made him the go-to guy for the many Spanish-speaking players on the team too.

Because baseball came to Japan from the United States, many of the terms are easily recognizable to English speakers as transliterations into Japanese from English. This is true for terms like ホームラン (*homuran*) for "home run," ボール (*boru*) for "ball," and バント (*bantu*) for "bunt." Others are also transliterations but more difficult to recognize. For instance, キャッチボール (*kyacchiboru*) is "to play catch." If you say it aloud a couple of times you might recognize its origin as "catch a ball." And if you are a real baseball buff (or a very lucky guesser), you might be able to make out ゲッツー (*gettsu*) as "get two" or "double play."

The perks of Nimura's job are not just linguistic in nature. Consider the fact that pitcher Ramon Troncoso invited Nimura to be the best man at his wedding. And Manny Ramirez (yes, *that* Manny Ramirez) insisted that Nimura be counted as part of the team when it came to signing baseballs. "Those are my favorite moments," Nimura says. Indeed, many young kids would say that those moments are the stuff of dreams.

Perfect Pitch

In 2009, a mistranslation cost Cuba the use of two of its pitchers at the World Baseball Classic in an elimination game against Mexico. The baseball tournament had guidelines for the limits of individual pitchers, but the guidelines were mistranslated from English into Spanish. Instead of indicating that no reliever could pitch the day after he had thrown thirty or more pitches (*treinta o más*), the translation in Spanish said more than thirty pitches (*más que trienta*). As a result, the Cuban manager removed two relievers after they had delivered exactly thirty pitches, wanting to keep them available to pitch the next day. Unfortunately, they were in fact ineligible to pitch—and none of the other teams had relied on the mistranslated text aside from Cuba.

Soccer Stars in Nightgowns

Brazil is known the world over for the ethnic, religious, and racial diversity of its people. But language and sport are two of the very few things that unite almost all the country's inhabitants. So when you translate the words that appear in the soccer section of one of Brazil's most popular newspapers, the stakes are high. There is no escape from scrutiny with the members of this audience, most of whom have been living and breathing soccer since birth.

"The Brazilian reader of the soccer pages is extremely demanding," explains Luciano Monteiro, a translator who specializes in soccer.[11] "He spends hours each day arguing about it with a passion that he will never have for politics, economics, or religion." According to Luciano, the reader will open the newspaper not only to learn the news but to validate his own opinions about the game. "Brazil is a country of two hundred million soccer coaches. Everyone claims to be an expert."

The minute the Brazilian soccer fan opens the newspaper—or increasingly, the web browser—he can easily spot the nonexpert writer. When it comes to soccer, any awkward phrasing or dullness in the text immediately jumps off the page. Obvious statements are not taken kindly, because the Brazilian fan does not want to be lectured. Sometimes, providing too much context can make the reader feel offended, as in, "Who do they think they are writing for? Someone who doesn't know soccer?"

Translators for Brazilian Portuguese do most of their work in the local market within Brazil. Even though soccer is also popular in Portugal, European Portuguese varies significantly from the Portuguese used in Brazil. For example, players from Portugal use the word *camisola* for "jersey," whereas in Brazil it means "nightgown." The word *balneário* means "locker room" in Portugal, but in Brazil it means a "seaside resort, a spa, or a beach town." Many a Brazilian has had a chuckle upon hearing a journalist from Portugal explain that the soccer players from his homeland are "headed to the spa in their nightgowns" during half time.

Of course, the need for translation in soccer extends beyond just the realm of news. Communications between players, agents, and FIFA agencies must be translated back and forth each day. Often, communications involve things like contracts that have been signed but not enforced and demands for payment of penalty fees. Usually, these projects are urgent matters, so the translation is often required with a very fast turnaround.

But the most visible of all translation work by far is the type that goes out to the masses. In Brazil, soccer unites all walks of life. So while other types of soccer-related projects have their challenges, as Luciano explains, "Soccer-related writing in Brazil has to accommodate both the semi-illiterate readers and the ones who are highly educated." The translation, like the writing, must use language that every reader can understand, to reflect the all-encompassing social phenomenon that defines the country.

Luckily, there is one word that requires no translation: *Gooo-ooooooooooooal!*

Translating Trash Talk at the World Cup

More than a quarter of a million foreign visitors descended upon South Africa for the 2010 World Cup—including fans, referees, members of the media, and teams from thirty-two countries speaking seventeen different languages. As with most international sporting events, the World Cup always presents plenty of multilingual communication challenges.

The organizers went to great lengths to arrange for interpreters for all the languages spoken by the visiting teams. In spite of these efforts, some interpreting snafus still took place. One of the most embarrassing translation-related moments was when FIFA provided an interpreter for a press conference with the team from Slovenia. There was just one problem—the interpreter spoke Slovak, which is spoken in Slovakia, not Slovenia. Teams from both countries were at the tournament, accounting in part for the mix-up. The Slovenes didn't find it very funny. (Apparently, this wasn't the first time the Slovenian team had been given a Slovak interpreter by mistake.)

Even when the languages are matched up correctly, the interpreter's job is never easy, with both fans and competitors hanging onto every word as anticipation builds before a match. When Slovene midfielder Andrej Komac said, "*Gremo na zmago*" (We are going for the win), his interpreter rendered it in a slightly different way, saying, "We are going to win." Because the interpreter's rendition was more definitive, his opponents thought Komac was trash-talking.

Komac wasn't the only victim of a mistranslation during the South African World Cup. Germany's coach Joachim Löw said: "*Wir wollen die Gegner spielerisch in Verlegenheit bringen*" (We want to outplay our opponents). Professional translations from German into English are not exactly hard to come by, but Löw's quote was mistranslated and published in the British media as saying that he wanted his team to "humiliate" and "embarrass" their opponents. (Of course, this might very well have been a reflection on the infamous British tabloid media rather than the translators.)

Even though Komac and Löw were not speaking ill of their competitors, it's common for players to curse during a game. As any soccer fan knows, referees can eject players for using obscene language. There were reports in the media that the referees in South Africa were given lists of curse words to memorize in all seventeen languages spoken by players at the World Cup. FIFA denied the reports, but some referees who speak English as a second language went on record to say that they had to spend some time getting familiar with the differences between British and American swear words.

Swear words and trash talk are not the only high-risk areas of translation at a sporting event. When a reporter asked Diego Maradona a question about his affectionate habit of kissing and hugging his team members, Maradona took it to mean that the reporter was insinuating that he was homosexual. He began to defend himself, saying, "I like women," and went on to describe his girlfriend's appearance. As often happens, the interpreter was blamed for the confusion, even though the reporter's question was rendered correctly to Maradona.

A lot of the translation work that took place for the World Cup in South Africa never made it in front of the camera crews—it happened well before the media arrived. Everything from tourist brochures, phrase books, advertisements, and South African–language booklets had to be translated. A multilingual country, South Africa has eleven official languages of its own—Afrikaans, English, Ndebele, Northern Sotho, Sotho, Swazi, Tswana, Tsonga, Venda, Xhosa, and Zulu—so many documents and written materials were translated not only into the languages of the participating teams but into the official tongues as well.

Signage and way-finding materials had to be translated too. These items are critical to help the international players, organizers, and spectators get to the right locations. The signs were not only multilingual but multicultural. One sign showed a list of prohibited items that could not be brought into the stadium. As with stadiums in most countries, the sign depicted things like motorcycle helmets and umbrellas. But as a clear reminder that the event was taking place in South Africa, the sign also showed pictures of Zulu shields and spears.

Ke Nako Needs No Translation

The South African character of the World Cup was definitely reflected in the language. For example, the Sotho expression *ke nako*, which means "it's time," appeared in the official slogan: "*Ke Nako*. Celebrate Africa's Humanity." When the slogan was translated into other languages, the phrase was left in-language:

Ke Nako. Célébrons l'esprit de l'Afrique. (French)
Ke Nako. Erlebe Afrikas Herzlichkeit. (German)
Ke Nako. Celebremos el espíritu africano. (Spanish)

Sometimes, a term or phrase is so special or unique that it doesn't require translation. That was the case with *ke nako*, as well as another term from South Africa that remained untranslated, and that the world is unlikely to ever forget—*vuvuzela*.

Interpreter Wins in Knockout

Interpreters don't often show up in sports headlines. But after the disputed title fight between Manny Pacquiao and Juan Márquez in November 2011, the *Washington Times* ran this caption over its story: "Undisputed Winner in Pacquiao vs. Márquez III: HBO's Interpreter Jerry Olaya."[12] On that particular day at work, Olaya was doing more than just his job as an interpreter, though that work alone earns him accolades from fans. In fact, his existing relationship with Márquez's camp may well have helped revive the canceled postfight interview with a disappointed and upset fighter. While this behind-the-scenes mediation would typically go unnoticed, in this case it allowed the more than 1.3 million Pay-Per-View customers on HBO to freely choose their own allegiances rather than draw conclusions based on an interview in broken English or no comments at all.

Does a boxing interpreter ever get dealt a blow that bewilders him? Not the physical kind. However, when Olaya's own boxing hero Miguel Cotto unexpectedly lost an epic fight against Antonio Margarito in July 2008, he was momentarily too stunned to continue. "It took me a little while to regain focus," he admits, but he was able to recover his composure and professionalism quickly enough to continue interpreting.[13]

Transferring some of the boxing terminology between Spanish and English is rather straightforward. For example, the term *knockout* sounds nearly the same in Spanish but is spelled *nocaut*. Though the term for *referee* exists in Spanish (*árbitro*), in boxing it's more common to use the cognate *réferi*. Spanish also uses the English terms for *uppercut*, *ringside*, and *jab*. The term *cut man*, which refers to the person whose job it is to stop the bleeding from boxers' cuts, also remains in English. And though one word for boxing in Spanish is *pugilismo* (similar to the English term *pugilism*), most people use *boxeo* instead.

The hardest part about interpreting in boxing is not necessarily the boxing-related terminology, although a tremendous amount of knowledge is certainly required for medical and technical terms. Instead, the most difficult part may be seamlessly switching between different types of interpreting in the interviews with boxers after the fight is over. Sometimes, the interpreter will render questions from a journalist by listening in one language and speaking the message in another (simultaneous interpreting). Other times, the interpreter has to listen to long segments first, commit them to memory, wait for a pause, and then interpret (consecutive interpreting). Many interpreters are adept at both types of interpreting, but interpreters in most other settings do not usually switch between them so quickly. Much like a boxer, who must remain light on his (or her) feet and quick to react with just the right move, so Olaya must react with his skills as an interpreter.

Swifter, Higher, Stronger . . . Louder?

London. Beijing. Athens. Sydney. Atlanta. Barcelona. Seoul. These are some of the cities that have hosted the most recent Summer Olympic Games, in which athletes from more than two hundred different nations participate. That's a lot of countries, which means a lot of languages, which means—you guessed it—a lot of translation and interpreting.

"People assume that interpreting for sports is easy. It's not," explains Bill Weber, chief interpreter for the Olympic games.[14] "In the summer, there are twenty-eight different sports, and interpreters have to prepare for all of them." There are four hundred different disciplines within those sports. In other words, Weber has to find interpreters who can render words like *tiller* (archery), *klaxon* (water polo), and *back kip* (gymnastics) with the same ease as they interpret terms like *clove hitch* (sailing), *sculling oar* (rowing), and *fetlock* (equestrian events).

But even the mastery of two languages is not enough to meet the standards for Olympic interpreters set by Weber, who speaks six languages with varying degrees of fluency. The interpreters he recruits need to have two sets of languages—active and passive. In a passive language, an interpreter can listen to and understand information in order to convey it into an active language, which is one they also speak fluently. Weber rarely recruits interpreters who have just one language combination. Ideally, they need to have at least two languages and a string of passive languages. This enables them to interpret in more directions, and for more athletes.

It can be a challenge for interpreters to speak as the athletes speak, using less formal terminology. Many of these interpreters are not athletes themselves—they work primarily as conference interpreters, so they are more accustomed to the long-winded sentences of political speeches than the comparatively concise language of athletes. Because of this, interpreters have to refrain from using the high-level language they are used to using, which is more difficult than it might seem.

The group of interpreters that Weber oversees is quite an elite one, and it changes somewhat with each Olympic Games. Because English and French are the two official languages of the Olympics, the team of interpreters is smaller when the host city is located in a country in which the members of the media speak either of these languages. For the Olympics in London, only about eighty interpreters were needed for Weber's team. For Beijing, two hundred were required because Chinese is not an official language.

But what about all the communication that takes place when the camera isn't rolling? In addition to the interpreters who work with Weber, there are typically between four thousand and ten thousand volunteer interpreters who work everywhere from the multilingual help desks to the playing fields. A tremendous number of other language services are used as well, such as telephone interpreting—used whenever an Olympian, family member, or staff member needs to communicate via telephone—or written translation—required for everything from the restaurant menus at the Olympic Village to the signs on bathroom doors.

Fire Exting Atcher

China has always had a problem with signs for foreigners written in less-than-perfect English. However, before the Olympics, Beijing decided to wage a major campaign to purge the city of imperfect English. Was it successful? One year after the Olympics took place, tourists visiting Beijing were still snapping photos of signs with such memorable phrases as, "Do not put toilet pepper in toilet," and a glass case holding a fire extinguisher brightly painted with the words, "Fire exting atcher box."[15]

CHAPTER 7

Connecting the World and Advancing Technology in Translation

Language is a great force of socialization,
probably the greatest that exists.

—Edward Sapir,
American linguist and anthropologist

Tweet Me in St. Louis . . . or Cairo . . . or Islamabad

Imagine inadvertently posting an update on a social media platform about the sound of a helicopter, without knowing that you had just alerted the world of the military raid on the Osama bin Laden compound. That's what Shohaib Athar did from his home in Pakistan.

Or consider Wael Ghonim, an Egyptian who was a prominent online activist for the prodemocracy movement in his home country. On January 26, 2011, he posted a status update, "I said one year ago that the Internet will change the political scene in Egypt and some friends made fun of me." One day later, he was detained and blindfolded for organizing protests. In Tahrir Square, his name appeared on many posters as people gathered to protest his disappearance. After twelve days, he was released.

Take into account Julia Probst, a German soccer fan who is deaf.

After she reads the lips of players and coaches, she tweets what they are saying, giving other fans access to inside details that are not broadcast on television.

In another instance, when a 7.2 magnitude earthquake took place in Turkey, television news anchor Okan Bayulgen received a message on his social network about two people who were trapped. He sent emergency information to relief workers. Within two hours, they had dug through the rubble and rescued the pair.[1]

There has been much press in Western media describing the role of social networks in helping communities connect, especially in regard to recent uprisings in places like Egypt, Syria, Tunisia. And in fact, these four stories all happened thanks to Twitter. While social networks give them a platform that enables them to connect, it's important to keep in mind that it's the people—the members of these online communities—who actually make things happen. To put things in perspective, journalists rarely do stories crediting AT&T and Verizon with saving countless lives every day via 911 calls.

What these platforms should truly be praised for is not for merely existing but for broadening their networks to make it possible for more people to use them and expanding the potential of global communication. For that to happen, these networks have to be made available in more languages. And that's exactly what Twitter is doing.

"By end of the first quarter of 2012, Twitter will be available in twenty-eight languages," explains Laura Gómez, localization manager at Twitter.[2] "Our goal is to build tools to make it easier for users to translate in their language—and have wider language coverage across the world." Indeed, those Twitter users all over the globe have helped the company translate its platform into their languages. Using a community model since 2009, the volunteer translators submit translations that are then voted on by the local translation groups.

Translation is important to Twitter's overall corporate strategy. "At the core of our mission is our longing to make Twitter accessible to everyone on the planet. In order for us to achieve this, we need to offer our tools and platforms in a user's native language, whenever possible," Gómez says. We want users to understand and participate in the global conversation while easily navigating through our product." The plan seems to be working. As of January 2012, Twitter had half a million volunteer translators and a small team of moderators who focus on quality control.

Community translation—working with volunteer users who are motivated to use Twitter in their native languages—also enables Twitter to launch new languages quickly. "Twitter in Simplified Chinese was translated and moderated in four days," Gómez explains. "This was part of a longer process that included building a community, establishing a relationship with the community moderators, agreeing on language guidelines and a basic glossary, as well as working on the specific challenges of every language."

"Our translators and moderators are proud of their individual contributions; they take their roles very seriously. Their commitment shows in our product," Gómez comments. Much like laying phone lines back in the early days of telephones, Twitter's volunteer translators are building the social network foundation that allows the Shohaib Athars, Wael Ghonims, Julia Probsts, and Okan Bayulgens of the world to make their voices heard.

Twitter's Additions to the World's Vocabulary

While purists often bemoan the creation of new words, it's actually a sign that languages are surviving and evolving to reflect a changing world. For example, the Welsh language recently added a new verb—*trydaru* for "to tweet"—because of Twitter's rapid growth in popularity. Terms for "to tweet" are now quite common in every market where Twitter has seen success, though some languages have employed the tried-and-true strategy of simply turning the product name into a verb (German users prefer to *twittern* rather than to *tweeten*, just as English users like *to google* or *to skype*), and Turkish Twitter users creatively prefer to *tweetle*. As if these new terms weren't enough, many languages have also adopted new terms for "retweet," which is when one person sends the same message another user sent previously via Twitter. Other languages have elected to keep it simple, using terms that just mean "resend" or "send again."

Wikipedia's 284 Languages (and Counting)

If content is king, as Bill Gates famously wrote back in 1996, Wikipedia expands the boundaries of the kingdom. How? By being among the earliest organizations on the Internet to offer information in other languages. And oh, what a lot of languages Wikipedia has available—a whopping 284 as of early 2012.[3] However, translation plays a different role from what you might imagine.

Like Twitter, Wikipedia relies on the volunteers in its global community. There are about a hundred thousand people who actively volunteer their time to edit and change Wikipedia pages. While not all of them are translators, many of them speak more than one language. None of the independent language versions of Wikipedia is a copy of another. Each version is an independent cultural work, created by communities of volunteers. It isn't uncommon for a volunteer to contribute to Wikipedias in several languages.

Of course, there are times when users choose to translate a Wikipedia article instead of writing a brand-new one from scratch. "Translation is more common for core sciences and mathematics," explains Jay Walsh.[4] "The most basic articles in English in these topic areas tend to be very high quality, so it's more common for Wikipedias in emerging languages to go to those areas for more direct, traditional translation." Walsh also points out that the projects that have been around the longest—those in languages like English, French, German, and Spanish—tend to have the more detailed and higher-quality articles that end up getting translated into projects for languages that are younger to Wikipedia. "We need more participants in less represented languages online, particularly as we see a sharp increase in the number of people coming online from non-English-speaking countries, particularly the global south," he remarks. Indeed, unique visitor data from third-party comScore shows a significant increase in Wikipedia's traffic in the global south, which typically refers to developing countries in the Southern Hemisphere.[5] What does it take for Wikipedia to get a new language off the ground? Language communities within Wikipedia generally want to create their own projects in their own languages. Using automatic translation tools to translate content from other Wikipedias is possible but does not always work very well. "Efforts to machine-translate Wikipedia articles and then bring in volunteers to build on top of those machine translations have not been particularly successful," Jay explains.

Wikipedia currently boasts more than twenty million articles across all languages. Most of its new content growth comes from the non-English projects. Many of these languages have millions of speakers. Take India, for example, which has more than a billion people, and 29 languages with more than a million native speakers, according to India's 2001 census. Another 60 languages have more than a hundred thousand speakers and 122 languages more than ten thousand native speakers. However, in spite of the plethora of other languages, Walsh observes that, "In India, the web tends to be English-rich, and Indic languages are far less present. Considering the fact that there are hundreds of millions of people there, a significant percentage of whom are not English speakers, it's safe to say that there is a serious lack of information available in Indic languages."

Indeed, the Tamil Wikipedia is the ninth most popular Tamil-language website in terms of traffic, while the Bangla Wikipedia contains the largest corpus of information in modern Bangla. As of October 2011, Wikipedia recorded 43.5 million page views in Indian-language wikis. As the communities continue to add new content, Wikipedia will continue to grow, and more people will have access to information in their mother tongues.

The communities of people who volunteer their time and expertise to the many Wikipedias of the world in hundreds of languages are building an important base of knowledge, one that may actually help the erosion of some less common languages. Translation plays a part in allowing that to happen. In turn, Wikipedia is also frequently used as a resource by professional translators.

Languages by the Numbers

This may surprise you: The ten languages with the most first-language speakers are (in order of number of speakers) Chinese, Spanish, English, Bengali, Hindi/Urdu, Arabic, Portuguese, Russian, Japanese, and German.[6] Which languages have the most content on the Internet? In order: English (with more than 50 percent), Chinese, Spanish, Japanese, Portuguese, German, Arabic, French, Russian, and Korean.[7] In other words, to achieve a balance of in-language web content that is proportional to the number of speakers, Chinese and Spanish will need to someday surpass English online. Meanwhile, Bengali and Hindi/Urdu still have a long digital road ahead.

Linking in Language

If you've searched for a job in the last several years, chances are you have a LinkedIn profile. As of early 2012, the professional networking site reported more than 120 million registered users in more than two hundred countries around the world. Many social networking sites enable you to connect with friends and family. A network like LinkedIn serves a slightly different purpose—to connect with people who can help you get ahead in your career. As business has grown to be more global in nature, building links to colleagues, customers, and business partners in other countries is not only more commonplace than ever before—it's more important for your career.

As of February 2012, LinkedIn was available in sixteen languages: English, Czech, Dutch, French, German, Indonesian, Italian, Japanese, Korean, Malay, Portuguese, Romanian, Russian, Spanish, Swedish, and Turkish. Why should you care? Nico Posner, principal product manager, international at LinkedIn, is well suited to answer that question.[8] He explains, "Whenever we add a new language to LinkedIn, our existing (usually multilingual) members in countries where that language is spoken broaden out their LinkedIn network to include those who only speak the newly added language."

In other words, each time LinkedIn has a launch in another language, the overall size of its network increases. And along with it, so do your opportunities for business introductions and job offers. While it's true that many businesspeople around the world speak English, they are more likely to add contacts if they can use a website in their native language. How much does translation contribute to the growth of the network? "To date, whenever we have launched LinkedIn in a new language, the rate of new member sign-ups has grown by at least double in that country after launch, sometimes by much more," Posner points out. Investors, take note. Adding languages is often a predictor of international revenue growth—not just for LinkedIn, but for other companies, too.

As the LinkedIn network has grown to encompass users who speak more languages, the company launched a feature to encourage members to post their profiles in other languages, too. "A multilingual profile makes you more visible and valuable," comments Posner. How so? Essentially, having a profile in multiple languages makes it more likely for it to be returned in search results—not only on LinkedIn, but in search engines such as Bing or Google.

If you watch the job boards, you'll notice that LinkedIn hires full-time translators, which helps fuel its international growth. Translation is an important part of the company's strategy—just as it is for most social networks. "If you can't read it, most likely you can't use it," Posner explains. "No matter how cool, useful, or popular a website may be, the products and services offered cannot be used or bought in a safe, effective, and meaningful way on an international scale without translation."

Ideas Worth Spreading Beyond English

Eighteen minutes. That's the maximum time available to deliver a TED talk. But it's a talk that will likely be watched by hundreds of millions of people around the world. If you've never seen a TED talk before, be prepared to get addicted. Imagine a collection of some of the world's most dynamic speakers, sharing their thoughts on their life's work in less than twenty minutes. Steve Jobs was among them, and it's exactly that sort of "brainiac charisma" that characterizes most of TED's speakers. The organization's mission is to share ideas that can change the world.

In the not-too-distant past, you'd have had to pay hundreds (if not thousands) of dollars to travel to a conference and bear witness to ideas like these, communicated by experts in every conceivable field of human knowledge. After taking time away from work and checking your bank balance, how many events could you realistically afford to travel to each year? One, maybe two? Now, picture yourself living in Swaziland. Or Laos. Or Nicaragua. And imagine that you don't speak English. What would your hopes be of ever attending such talks, let alone understanding them?

TED has solved both of those problems. Its thought-provoking talks are available to anyone with access to the Internet. Perhaps even more important, they are on offer in a whopping ninety-one languages, and rising fast.[9] And that's where translation comes in. Go to the TED website, and you can find talks that have been subtitled by an impressive seventy-five hundred registered volunteer translators.[10]

How did the project start? "Soon after we made TED talks available for the first time, people around the world began approaching us to see if they could subtitle the talks into other languages so they could be shared," explains Kristin Windbigler, Open Translation Project manager at TED.[11] She points out that these enthusiastic individuals were not requesting TED to provide the subtitles; instead, they were volunteering to do it. "We heard this request over and over again, from dozens of people around the world, many of whom began subtitling talks on their own, just to share them with friends," Windbigler points out. The requests were so persistent that TED knew it had to take them seriously. So the organization set about building a system that would allow volunteers to subtitle the talks in other languages.

And the system works. More than a thousand talks have been translated, and 20 percent of all TED talk video views come from people watching with subtitles enabled. Volunteers translate TED talks into languages as diverse as Bislama, spoken natively by six thousand people in Vanuatu, and Hupa, a Native American language with less than two thousand speakers. On the other hand, you'll also find plenty of translated talks that are available in languages with enormous populations, such as Malayalam, the mother tongue of thirty-six million people in India, and Khmer, with fifteen million speakers in Cambodia.

But just because a language is widely spoken does not mean that it's always easy to obtain information in it. Let's consider Arabic, which has more than three hundred million native speakers. Arabic is a language that is growing in importance in the world. With more and more people obtaining access to the Internet each day, its growth rate is outpacing many other languages.

In fact, one of the most prolific translators in the TED community speaks Arabic as his mother tongue. His name is Anwar Dafa-Alla, and he lives in Sudan. The talk that first inspired Dafa-Alla to translate with the goal of sharing it with others in his country and continent was called "African Einstein" by Neil Turok. It was the first of many talks that he would watch. As of December 2011, he had worked on more than 685 TED talks into Arabic.[12] The process TED uses requires one person to translate the talks and a second person to review the translations to make sure they are accurate. Dafa-Alla used to translate the majority of the talks into Arabic himself, but now he mostly reviews the translations of others. He speaks not only Arabic and English, but Korean—he's obtaining his PhD in South Korea—and he works as a university professor in Sudan.

Why does someone like Dafa-Alla donate his time and translation skills to TED? Like many of the volunteers, he is hungry for knowledge. "TED speakers are usually at the cutting edge of their fields and their technologies," he explains. This can make the translation especially challenging. "You often end up coining new terms in Arabic, or coming up with a creative approach to the terminology. At the same time, you need to make sure that it can be understood by the average, everyday speaker."

But his own thirst for information is not the only motivator. Dafa-Alla wants to make sure others can also benefit from new ideas. At the same time, he also wants to make sure that the voices of Arabic speakers are heard. "We need to tell our own stories of our own lives, so that other people can learn from those stories too."

Apparently, Dafa-Alla's underlying reasons for volunteering are similar to those of other translators who volunteer for TED. "They care deeply about making the world a better place. The democratization of ideas is very important to them," Windbigler points out. After all, if the mission of TED is to share ideas that can change the world, translation spreads those ideas even further. One can only hope that, as time goes on, more and more TED talks will be available in languages that are subtitled *into* English instead. After all, great ideas can come from anywhere.

Friends with Translation Benefits

When you write on someone's wall, accept a friend request, or update your timeline, you probably don't think for a second about translation. Yet, translation has played a critical role in Facebook's history—and continues to fuel its ongoing global expansion. As of late 2011, there were more than eight hundred million users of Facebook. In a world of seven billion people, that means that more than one in every ten people is a member of the world's largest social network. That kind of global growth doesn't just happen by accident.

Back in 2007, Facebook started trying out an experimental method of translation. It decided to engage the crowd, to allow its users to determine how they would like to see the site translated into their languages. Facebook users rallied in support of the cause. Within just a couple of weeks of starting the effort, they launched the first language, Spanish. Envision a tiny snowball at the top of the mountain. Users responded with positive feedback, so the company opened up its crowdsourcing platform to enable users to translate the site into French and German. Imagine the snowball beginning to roll down the mountain.

The following year, 2008, was the year of internationalization at Facebook. "One can argue that translations contributed the most growth," explains Ghassan Haddad, director of internationalization at Facebook.[13] He notes that the number of users in Italy skyrocketed following the launch of the Italian language, jumping from 375,000 to 933,000 in just four months. In France, during the three months following the release, the number jumped from 1.4 million to 2.4 million users. "This growth story was repeated in almost all locales," Haddad points out. But the growth was not just limited to the countries themselves. Speakers of French living in other countries also began joining Facebook as a result of the newly translated version. And so began the avalanche.

Facebook is currently available in seventy-seven languages, including U.S. English, and another thirty languages are in various phases of translation progress. The currently available languages represent over 90 percent of the world population and over 95 percent of people with access to the Internet. The company has continued to tap into its user base to produce the translated versions of its website. Facebook's crowdsourced translation model has since served as an example for many hundreds of organizations throughout the world, including various nonprofits and charitable organizations. In fact, there are now entire companies that make money from setting up such online communities and paying professional translators to provide the translations through these portals. "Since our users are major stakeholders and partners in the translation, the launchability of additional languages depends greatly on their involvement," Haddad observes. For example, in October 2011, a small group of Khmer speakers expressed deep interest in having Facebook in their language and began working extensively toward that goal. Just two months later, Facebook was officially launched in Khmer.

Of course, Facebook does not rely exclusively on volunteer translators to produce all its content in other languages. Approximately thirty languages are supported by professional (paid) translation providers. When professional translators originally learned that Facebook was using volunteers to do some of its translation work, they were outraged at first. They worried that it threatened their business model and that it would result in poor quality. The opposite happened. Not only was the quality high but the initial work of the volunteers led to paid translation work that otherwise would not have existed. But the challenges of managing all of the translated versions of the website extend far beyond just language. "Keeping all parts of the site translated at all times is a very challenging task, due to the fact that Facebook development moves very quickly," Haddad explains. "During crunch times, it's not unusual to see a churn of approximately ten percent or more of the site content in a single week."

Not only do Haddad and his team have to make sure that the translation is ready at the same time as the launch of the English version, but they have to mitigate security risks as well. They also have to maintain their own proprietary translation application, which enables their nonvolunteer translation team members—both in-house and contract based—to collaborate in real time.

For the community-translated languages, it's no easy undertaking for Facebook to manage such an enormous crowd of volunteers. Haddad and his team have to measure what parts of the site are most visible to users, warranting the earliest attention, and they have to direct translators to the user interface for those parts of the site. They also have to maintain a controlled environment to guard against people who might not be translating for the right reasons. "Over half a million users have contributed to translations on Facebook," he explains. "But there are hundreds, if not thousands of individuals who are there to produce everything from silly translations to downright malicious ones." Some users even attempt to sabotage the translations by typing in obscenities and ethnic slurs, so the environment Facebook has created must control the problems before they get out of hand.

Of course, even the best monitor at the high school gymnasium can't prevent the kids from pulling silly pranks. A group of Turkish Facebook users decided to replace several common phrases in Facebook with some "creatively" translated versions. For example, the Facebook chat notification "Your message could not be sent because the user is offline" was translated as: *Mesajın gönderilemedi çünkü penisin çok küçük*, which means "Your message could not be sent because you have a tiny penis."

What did Facebook users in Turkey think when this message suddenly appeared? They got a kick out of it, according to eighteen-year-old Facebook user Nuri Turkoglu. "That actually happened to one of my friends, not to me personally. But when we found out about it, we just laughed. It was hilarious," he shared. Turkoglu began using Facebook in Turkish, his native language, when he was in tenth grade in Turkey. But after spending time attending high school in the

United States, he now interacts with friends online in English, too. Though the languages are easy to navigate through Facebook's interface, cultural differences are still prominent. Turkoglu, a dual citizen of Turkey and the United States, points out that Americans and Turks use Facebook in very different ways: "Turkish people like to socialize and share more photos and videos with comments than Americans do." He also notices that the two cultures behave differently when using Facebook instant messaging. "Americans tend to write using plain text. It feels like you're just reading text from a book when chatting with them," he says. "Turks use more emoticons to express their feelings, which makes it much easier to understand what they are really trying to communicate."[14]

Facebook's stated mission is to make the world more open and connected. How does translation make it happen? As Haddad from Facebook remarks, "Language is the most critical enabler of communication. Without translation, connecting the world simply isn't possible." Even bilingual Facebook users like Turkoglu, who don't rely completely on translation but still use it to interact with friends in more than one language, would tend to agree.

To Unfriend, to Defriend, or to Remove Connections?

In 2009, the word *unfriend* was chosen as the *New Oxford American Dictionary*'s Word of the Year. Major media outlets did stories on the influence of Facebook, attributing the word to the social media giant. However, in reality, the word *unfriend* was never an official Facebook term. Facebook used *remove connection* instead, but the term *unfriend* became part of common parlance. Another advantage of the phrase *remove connection*? It's much easier to translate!

Òjò, Ọjọ, Ójó

You probably take it for granted that you can type on a keyboard in your native language. But what if you looked down at the keys and saw only foreign characters? English speakers are lucky to have such a keyboard-friendly language. Just twenty-six characters, ten digits, and a handful of punctuation and other marks were the only characters that had to fit on the original English-language typewriter. European languages like French, German, or Danish, with just a few special characters for umlauts or accented letters, were also fairly easy to accommodate.

But what about a language like Chinese—which has sixty thousand characters, thirty-five hundred of which are used in daily communication? Or South Asian languages like Thai and Indic languages? Cyrillic languages like Russian and Greek? And what about the right-to-left languages like Hebrew and Arabic?

When computers came into fashion, developers quickly found solutions for major languages by creating virtual keyboards within operating systems that could be mapped to the actual physical keyboards. In other words, typing on keys with Latin letters would produce Russian, Thai, or Hebrew characters on the screen. For languages like Chinese, programs were developed that allowed for screen-based selection of characters that were filtered on the basis of pronunciation or other characteristics.

So what about all the other languages? Consider languages like Yorùbá, Ìgbo, and Hausa, which are spoken by sixty-three million people in Nigeria. And these are just three of the more than two hundred languages of Nigeria that have a written form. (If you think two hundred written languages is a lot, just consider the fact that the total number of languages *spoken* in Nigeria is a mind-boggling 510.) These three languages, most of which are based on a Latin alphabet system, do not lend themselves to a keyboard because of special letters and a plethora of diacritical marks above or below the characters. For instance, using the Yorùbán *álífábẹ́ẹ̀tì* (alphabet), the word *ojo* with different diacritics could mean any of the following: "rain" (*òjò*), "day" (*ọjọ*), or "uncourageous" (*ójó*). As recently as just a few years ago, authors writing in Yorùbá had to type out texts on an English typewriter or computer and then pass the texts on to secretaries, who would then add the missing marks by hand.

Adé Oyégbọla and his partner Olúkáyọdé Olúwọlé wanted to find a solution to this problem. Inspired in the late 1990s by their inability to find a keyboard to adequately create business cards in their native language of Yorùbá, they decided to create an input system that would cover not just their mother tongue, but all the written languages of Nigeria.[15] They created a keyboard that was very similar to the English keyboard, to make the transition from the familiar environment as easy as possible.

In addition, they also provided access to all of Nigeria's necessary extra letters by creating a second set of shift keys with which users were able to add diacritical marks to any of the characters. The resulting product, the Kọnyin Multilanguage Keyboard, is used by various government agencies, universities, religious groups, and translators. Even companies like Dell and HP are looking into the underlying drivers that make the use of these keyboards possible.

Oyégbọla explains his motivation for creating and distributing the new keyboards as follows: "The very survival of these languages is at stake." He believes that improving the ability of his fellow Nigerians, many of whom have been computer illiterate, to type in their native languages on a computer will go far toward preserving their culture, their identity, and their most fundamental mode of communication.

As translators, we see yet another benefit. The easier it gets for people to communicate in their native languages, the more readily translators can transfer information into and out of those languages, thus connecting a country and its people to the rest of the world.

Tools of the Trade

Translators are accustomed to using various keyboard systems to input languages into their computers. Until recently, however, the writing systems of many languages could not be combined within a single document. While we had software that supported the individual writing systems of most major languages, it wasn't possible to combine Chinese and Thai, Arabic and Hebrew, or Japanese and Russian in a single document or web page. Talk about frustrating.

Then came Unicode. A system whose development started in the 1990s, it can now encode far more than a hundred thousand characters from virtually all living and many dead written languages. It also includes mathematical symbols, musical annotation marks, emoticons, and many other writable characters. It's a translator's nirvana.

Translators' use of technology doesn't stop there. There's a whole software industry that addresses the needs of professional translators in most fields—especially those working with technical, medical, legal, and business-focused texts.[16]

One of the most important technology tools for translators is called "translation memory." Think of it as a high-end consignment shop: It's a database that stores past translations for reuse rather than translating from scratch. As any good "thrifter" knows, there's a certain risk involved in the thrill of the hunt—the quality of the inventory goes down if the translation wasn't good to start with or if the same sentence should be translated differently in a different context. Hardly any translations are suited to all occasions—like showing up for a picnic wearing a tuxedo. For this reason, many translators prefer to shop their own closets first. If the database of past translations consists mostly of their own work, they can be assured of the quality, and they know how to mix and match them.

Another technology translators use is called a *termbase*. Termbases are also databases, but they contain more detailed data, with lots of descriptive information about each term such as definitions, grammatical information, explanations of when to use or avoid using a specific term, and possible synonyms. A termbase is less like a brick-and-mortar consignment shop and more like eBay, with lots of product information at your fingertips. Translation is rarely a one-to-one paradigm, in which a word in one language perfectly matches a word in another language. Terms can be translated in myriad ways, and a termbase helps us choose the correct translation for each context. And just like translation memories, termbases can be shared among many translators working in real time in virtual teams.

Finally, some translators also use machine translation, in which a software program or online tool automatically translates the text according to its own set of rules. Believe it or not, this can sometimes require more work than translating from scratch, because we still need to do intensive editing to clean things up afterward. Perhaps our analogy here might be a personal shopper. If someone else buys them, you'd have no guarantee that the clothes would fit the required size or style, so you might end up with a lot of costly alterations before you could actually use them.

Yet for some projects, companies just want an approximate translation—they don't care if the clothes fit perfectly, so long as they can be worn. For these projects, we human translators train the translation programs, teach them the correct vocabulary, and tweak their understanding of grammar. Automated translation does have its place, especially in certain industries. For example, in the legal field, machine translation is often used to mine extensive amounts of data, such as case law, to flag items that might be relevant for attorneys working on a given case. In the manufacturing sector, machine translation is sometimes used for the extensive support content and documentation that often has a high degree of predictable structure and repeated terms and phrases. In these instances, automated translation does not replace human translation. It serves a different purpose, but it still requires professional translators.

Microsoft, Māori, and Plenty of *Pūmanawa*

Most computer users have one very basic requirement: the language their computer speaks needs to be in their own native tongue. The computer communicates with us in the form of dialog boxes, menus, and error messages, and most of those little messages are brought to us by a software company that is represented on the majority of the world's computers: Microsoft.

It's a company that's been remarkably multilingual. The 2010 version of its operating system—Windows 7—was released in thirty-six different languages. An impressive number indeed, but is it sufficient? Well, no, not if you want to support language communities that don't speak one of those languages as their primary language.

In 2001, to respond to those unmet language needs, Microsoft's Local Language Program began to call on communities of languages without access to localized versions of the software to produce Language Interface Packs, appropriately abbreviated as LIPs, that would provide translations to the most commonly used parts of the software (approximately 80 percent of the user interface). For Windows 7 there are now sixty LIPs available in total. This batch covers languages from Afrikaans to Catalan to Inuktitut to Malayalam to Punjabi and Yorùbá.

Māori, an official language spoken in New Zealand by between 60,000 and 120,000 of the country's native people, is one of these languages. For the Māori LIP project, Microsoft enlisted the help of Māori language activist Dr. Te Taka Keegan, a man with a fervent belief in the need to open up the modern world to the ancient language of Māori.[17] This conviction is deeply rooted in history. Indeed, the Māori people—and the country of New Zealand—have suffered long-lasting consequences as a result of outsiders "assisting" with important language-related matters affecting their people.

Back in 1840, the British government and Māori chiefs assembled to debate the Treaty of Waitangi, a document the leaders hoped would end years of bloodshed and determine the future of New Zealand. The night before, the document had been handed off to Henry Williams, a British missionary and Bible translator, so that he could translate it from English into Māori. Helped by his son, he rushed to get the translation completed in time. The next morning, the treaty was read aloud in both languages. Unfortunately, it contained an error that would change the course of history.[18]

In the text of the original English treaty, the Māori were asked to "cede to Her Majesty the Queen of England absolutely and without reservation all the rights and powers of Sovereignty." This was translated into Māori as "*ka tuku rawa atu ki te Kuini o Ingarani ake tonu atu te Kawanatanga.*" The last word of the Māori translation (*Kawanatanga*) does not mean "sovereignty," but "governance" or "government." The Māori leaders, hoping for the installment of a legal system to protect them from lawless foreigners and restore order, were ready to allow the British Crown to take over *governance*. But they were not willing to sign away their *sovereignty* over their land. Yet that is exactly what happened. (There has been extensive debate over whether Williams's error was intentional or inadvertent.)

More than 130 years later, in 1975, the Waitangi Tribunal was formed and charged with recommending reparations to the Māori from the government of New Zealand. But nothing could ever repair the damage done by colonization, let alone restore the "stolen generations," to use the words of Chief Judge J. V. Williams.

Knowing full well the effects of these stolen generations on his culture as the direct result of a mistranslation, Keegan is focused on the generations of the future—only one in six Māori under the age of fifteen can speak the language fluently as of the 2006 census. Carla Hurd, who oversees Microsoft's Local Language Program, recalls conversations with children in other areas with LIP programs: "When they told me they didn't speak the language, and I asked them why, they said, 'You're not cool with your friends if you do. I only speak that with my grandma and grandpa.' Social media, texting, web surfing—these technologies are used by the younger generations. If they cannot use the language to do what's 'cool,' then the language will die."[19]

A lecturer at the University of Waikato, Keegan has dedicated much of his life to ensuring the survival of the language through technology. He previously helped Microsoft develop the Māori keyboard (which gives easy access to the long vowels with macrons, such as ō, ū, ā, or ē) and worked on various other high-tech and open-source projects. He helped a search engine provider localize its search interface and a translation platform into Māori, assisted with translations of the open source e-learning platform Moodle, and managed the project to digitize eighteen thousand legacy Māori newspaper pages. His ground-up approach looks for the projects and resources that will have the most impact on the Māori language and people.

The language of technology is often equated with the language of progress, but in many languages, terms for computing do not even exist. Why would they, if the people who speak the languages can't use computers in those languages? So, Keegan and his teams had to develop new terminology from scratch, which then had to be submitted to the Māori Language Commission for approval. For every new term, they tried to find traditional Māori words to describe the new technological concepts. For the term *software*, for instance, they used the traditional Māori term *pūmanawa*, which refers to talents and skills, things that aren't initially seen but become obvious when put into action. Only when the simplicity and clarity of the language becomes clouded with traditional terms did they revert to transliterations of the English terms in Māori. Terms for digital unit sizes like *byte*, *kilobyte*, and *megabyte* were transliterated as *paita*, *kiropaita*, and *mekapaita*. In other words, generations of Māori children will have Keegan and his team's *pūmanawa* (in the traditional sense) to thank for the *pūmanawa* they will be able to use (in the software sense). And this time around—unlike back in 1840—the future of the Māori people will be defined by translations that come from within their own community.

Beam Me Up, Babelfish

To find them, look no further than the "three stars"—*Star Wars, Star Trek,* and *Stargate.* You can also see them in *Doctor Who, Futurama,* and of course, *A Hitchhiker's Guide to the Galaxy.* We're talking about "universal translators," those futuristic machines designed to bridge language barriers between earthlings and aliens.

Speech translation is not just the stuff of science fiction. It exists today, and it's a field that is growing. But machines cannot yet fully replace humans when it comes to converting spoken language. A human can interpret simultaneously—listening and speaking at nearly the same time. For now, a machine works much more slowly. Actually, the machine has to complete three separate processes. First, a speech recognition program comprehends what was spoken in one language, converting it into text. Then, using automatic translation, the written text gets translated into a second language. For the final step, the machine vocalizes or speaks the translated version of the text.

Because there are so many variables involved, speech translation presents even more obstacles to developers than text translation. Humans are fairly adept at looking past a speech impediment or unfamiliar accent, but machines are not. Just consider the fact that when Apple launched Siri, which stands for Speech Interpretation and Recognition Interface, it had problems recognizing and interpreting Scottish accents. Non-Scottish humans may have problems deciphering Scottish accents, too, but humans are at least capable of making better guesses.

Humans also know to listen more intently when someone is whispering, but machines don't instinctively do this. Humans can block out sound from other sources—say, a baby crying in the background—but machines have a hard time with that. If there are two male voices speaking the same language, a human can usually discern between them quickly. Machines don't find it so easy.

But developers love a challenge, so there are plenty of speech translation products on the market. Google has added speech options to its core translation product. The U.S. Department of Defense has spent millions upon millions of dollars over the years on various projects to automate the translation of speech. There are some promising examples of technologies that do a decent job when limited to certain settings or specific languages. There are even some tools that work reasonably well (after significant time spent in training the speech recognition portion) with a single user's voice. Yet, despite plenty of investment from government organizations and private-sector firms, automated speech translation today does not even come close to doing what human interpreters can do.

Enabling human beings who speak different languages to communicate with each other in real time without relying on a human interpreter is one of the final frontiers of translation technology. Such an achievement would surely represent the fall of the figurative Tower of Babel. Will it ever happen? Maybe there's a reason the humans in the science fiction films and television shows always seem to speak the same language. Usually, they are also trapped in a linguistic time warp, speaking a form of American English that strangely ceased to evolve in the late twentieth and early twenty-first centuries. Perhaps it's easier for most people to imagine a world in which humans can seamlessly communicate with aliens than for them to imagine instantly overcoming human language barriers.

Speech translation will improve as time goes on. Of that we have no doubt. In fact, we can envision an array of possibilities for customization—for example, a technology that can translate from one generation to another. One that can detect and filter out statements that a listener might view as culturally inappropriate. One that slows down your speech and turns up the volume for an older person with hearing loss. One that fixes your stutter in real time. One that enables you to speak exclusively in rhyme. Or in the voice of your favorite actress. Or in a perky voice when you're feeling sick. All of these language preferences are possible in theory, but plain old translation from one spoken language to another is perhaps the most difficult of these to implement.

As long as human beings speak different languages, the need for translation will continue. And as long as translation exists—even if it someday becomes more fully automated—it will always require the skills, talent, and expertise of human specialists. After all, even in science fiction, someone has to build and maintain those universal translators. Indeed, Spock's famed lack of emotion was apparently due to a translation error. In the novel *Spock's World* by Diane Duane, Spock's mother, who helped build the universal translator, was blamed for a mistranslation that would cause Vulcans to be unfairly stereotyped. The Vulcan word *Arie'mnu*, which translates to "passion's mastery," was mistranslated by Spock's mom as "lack of emotions."

The Spirit Is Willing but the Translation Is Weak

Automatic web-based translation produces no shortage of hilari-ous translations. (For a high-tech version of the old telephone or gossip game, go to www.translationparty.com, a site that keeps on translating between Japanese and English until an equilibrium is reached.) One famous example of machine translation gone awry is actually an urban legend. As the story goes, the sentence "The spirit is willing, but the flesh is weak" was plugged into a machine translation system to be rendered into Russian. Allegedly, the com-puter produced "The vodka is strong, but the meat is rotten" in Rus-sian. This tale has never been substantiated, but it's not completely inconceivable. The story probably serves a good purpose as a warn-ing that generic machine translation cannot and should not be blindly trusted.

Parlez-Vous C++?

Anyone who's taken a language course in school knows how hard it is to learn a foreign language. And, depending on what language you speak natively, some languages are significantly harder than others. For example, it takes an estimated ten years to train an Arabic–English translator to reach full competence, a hard lesson the U.S. government learned after the events of 9/11.

Given this dismal statistic, then, it's all the more impressive to learn that a single group of folks in Mountain View, California, paved the way for carrying out virtually unlimited English–Arabic translation in a matter of months, in addition to more than sixty other languages with a total of more than four thousand language combinations. Funnily enough, the languages that unified this brainy team were C++ and Java, programming languages used by software engineers.

You probably guessed it: We're talking about the talented team behind Google Translate. When we sat down with Franz Och of the Google Translate team at its headquarters in Mountain View, he told us that in 50 percent of all Google searches for the word *translation*, users typed in the words "Google Translate."[20] This means that half of all Google users who are interested in translation automatically turn to the machine translation tool that Google offers. Surprised by that number? That probably just means you're a native (or competent) English speaker.

You see, if you search the web in English, you'll have no trouble finding content. Or if you're searching in French, German, Chinese, or many other major languages, the online world is your oyster. You can find information on virtually any topic. But what about the hundreds of millions of people who don't speak those languages? That's where services like Google Translate come in.

To translate all of the information on the web into and out of so many languages, Google doesn't follow the rules. Instead of relying on complex grammar rules that change from one language to the next, Google figures out the best way to translate a given phrase or paragraph by doing what it does best—crunching lots of numbers. This approach, known as statistical machine translation, feeds computers with very large amounts of language data. With the help of ever-more-sophisticated algorithms, the computers process these data and then employ them to emulate human language in translation. A company like Google naturally has access to two of the three main components of such a successful system—fast computers and lots of data. The third ingredient, a team of highly skilled computer engineers, wasn't difficult for them to assemble either.

The Google Translate team now finds that speakers of languages that are not yet offered often lobby for inclusion. Och explained that they are still developing engines for many languages, but there are essentially only two ways to make the cut. One way is to demonstrate an immediate need. When the earthquake hit Haiti in January of 2010, Google used materials collected by a team at Carnegie Mellon University and other sources to release a version of Haitian Creole within days. (Microsoft used the same material for its machine translation engine and released the Haitian Creole version at around the same time.) Though it wouldn't have passed the company's quality threshold under other circumstances, the subsequent widespread use by rescue personnel in Haiti justified the publication of a language that was still only at an alpha stage of testing.

Similarly, the Persian engine was released during the 2009 Iranian election protests, though it was also technically still in a pre-release state. Again, it was embraced immediately because, as Och points out, "When there's an option in an urgent situation between no translation and a gisted, or approximated, translation, the choice is clear."

Under calmer circumstances, Google employs the second criterion for releasing a language into public use: quality. To evaluate a language's translation quality, the team uses "language informants" as well as computerized evaluation criteria. Once a language is released, the refinement does not stop. New translated data are produced on an ongoing basis, whether in the form of random information on the web, books accessed through the Google Books program, or user-generated data through tools like Google Translator Toolkit, a tool that allows for the human translation of various document types. According to Och, this is a particularly relevant data source for languages with otherwise relatively little content on the web. The team employs everything that is deemed useful (with the exception of translations produced by Google's own or other machine translation programs) to continuously train existing and new engines.

And the results? It all depends on the language pair and the expectation. For language pairs like Serbian and Croatian or Hindi and Urdu, languages that are closely related, results might be stunningly good. English and Swedish? Portuguese and Spanish? There you also might find results of high quality. Other language combinations will likely provide a good general idea of what the original text says, which is great if that's what you're expecting.

We asked Och whether we would ever be able to apply the same quality expectations to Google Translate as we would to a qualified human translator. "Oh," he said with a grin, "maybe in twenty, or fifty, or in five hundred years." In the meantime, his team will keep working toward their next goal, an ambitious hundred languages, or ten thousand language pairs.

Who Needs Engineers?

"I'm bringing a translator and a security officer. Why would I need an engineer?" These were the words of the character named Archer in an episode of *Star Trek* that aired in 2001 (but took place in 2151). Truth be told, all computerized translation gadgets rely heavily on humans—both those with linguistic expertise and engineering know-how.

The Futurist Has Faith

Inventor and technologist Ray Kurzweil is probably best known throughout the world for his predictions about technology and how it will shape the future. At age fifteen, he wrote his first computer program. Before graduating from high school, he was invited to the White House and congratulated by President Lyndon B. Johnson for winning first prize in the International Science Fair for a computer he had built. In his books, *The Age of Spiritual Machines* and *The Singularity Is Near*, he talks about how machines will replace humans in a variety of areas.

What many people may not realize is that Kurzweil's long and impressive career in science and technology has been characterized by a close involvement with the arts. His father was a musician and his mother was a visual artist. That computer he created in high school? It composed music. Over the course of his career, he has developed a visual art synthesizer, a "cybernetic poet" that automatically generates poetry, and computer programs to assist the creative art process. In 1984, he unveiled an electronic synthesizer called the Kurzweil K250. In tests, musicians could not discern the difference between the synthesizer and a grand piano.

In other words, Kurzweil has devoted most of his life to automating processes and functions performed by humans, paying special attention to the arts. But when it comes to automating the art of translation, he doesn't think it will ever be fully possible. Kurzweil believes that society will get to a point at which computers have human levels of language understanding by 2029. He also believes that machines will eventually be able to translate information— both spoken and written—better than they do today. He points to the fact that automated translation options like Google Translate are already available on mobile phones. However, machine translation will never be perfect.

Many of the stories we've shared so far in this book make it clear that the tasks of translation and interpreting are extremely difficult to do well. That's precisely why human translators and interpreters need machines. These two professions have evolved over time, though perhaps not enough. Interpreters still have to rely on the terminology in their heads. Translators for most languages still depend largely on their own recollections of grammatical rules. Most interpreters and translators would actually benefit from getting *more* help from technology—not less—to make them more productive and improve the quality of their work.

When asked about whether machines will ever fully replace human interpreters and translators, Kurzweil points out the similarities with the field of music. When he invented his synthesizer in the 1980s, many musicians feared that they would be out of a job. He says, "I don't think these technologies so much replace whole fields, in general. What they do is replace, perhaps, a certain way of applying them." He points out that most of the jobs that exist in the world today didn't exist just a few decades ago. He believes that the actual translation and interpreting tasks performed by humans may evolve, but the demand for language services as a whole will only grow.[21]

The complexity of translation is not lost on Kurzweil—far from it. He goes so far as to say that the epitome of human intelligence is our ability to command language. He even characterizes translation as "the most high-level type of work one can imagine." Tools like machine translation, he says, will only boost humans' ability to use, transform, and manipulate language. And, as with many things in

Kurzweil's career, it all comes back to the arts. When asked how the language professions will evolve with technology, he says, "I think what we've seen already, in the music field, is a good model of that." The need for human musicians has not faded away in spite of advances in technology. Music continues to surround us and enrich our lives. So, too, will translation.

This book began with a dedication to translators and interpreters, and many of them have appeared as main characters in the stories we've shared. Now, as we end our journey, we thought you might like to know a bit more about how these often unsung heroes and heroines view their own work.

There are hundreds of thousands of translators and interpreters throughout the world. Their lives and work are as varied as the stories in this book. The situations they encounter, the languages they speak, and the places they work are tremendously diverse. To give you a better idea of what their jobs entail, we conducted an informal survey of people who work in these professions.

When we asked roughly twelve thousand translators and interpreters what they loved most about their work, they had plenty to say. Even at first glance, it's clear they enjoy their jobs. In fact, when we asked about their work satisfaction, 96.4 percent of respondents said that they were either "very satisfied" or "satisfied."

But how do they believe they transform the world? One translator wrote, "No one can know every language in the world, but our work makes it possible for people to read everything anyway." Another explained, "Because of my work as a translator of textbooks, children can learn in their native languages." A legal interpreter pointed out, "By preventing miscommunication, I am also preventing lawsuits," while a medical interpreter noted, "Medical interpreting improves public health." And one person who worked as both a translator and interpreter summarized, "Without translators and interpreters, there would be no trade agreements, no international business, no globalization."

We also asked these professionals to tell us about the most unusual assignments they had ever received. The responses included such diverse answers as "going on a drug bust with the police" to "translating the daily journals of French movie critics at Cannes" to "translating a crane operator's manual." Interpreters mentioned conveying the words of victims of trafficking, Nobel Prize winners, heads of state, and guests on *The Jerry Springer Show*. Translators mentioned converting Chinese phrases for tattoo parlors, due diligence documents for one of the largest business mergers in the twentieth century, and a survey about the usages of toilet paper.

Some mentioned translating love letters, while others had to translate correspondence for private investigators between a woman who was cheating on her husband and the man she was cheating with. One respondent had interpreted for Pope John Paul II, while another mentioned interpreting for Fidel Castro. One person mentioned interpreting for a routine medical procedure in which the patient unexpectedly died, while another mentioned interpreting as a baby came into the world.

We also asked translators and interpreters to do the ultimate in linguistic synthesis by picking a single word to describe their work. Some of the most common words they chose were *fascinating*, *challenging*, *intriguing*, and *rewarding*. A surprising number of them answered with the word *supercalifragilisticexpialidocious*. But many also selected words like *creative*, *exciting*, *empowering*, *engaging*, *engrossing*, *fulfilling*, *interesting*, *stimulating*, and *varied*.

While the results of our poll seem to indicate that these folks are a happy bunch, there is no denying that translators and interpreters work, for the most part, without much fanfare. And that's in spite of the important contributions they indisputably make to the world. Of those we surveyed, just one lone person selected a negative word to characterize their translation and interpreting work: *underappreciated*. Our sincerest hope is that, one reader at a time, this book will help to change that.

ACKNOWLEDGMENTS

A book like this, which encompasses so many lives, places, contexts, and languages, can be written only with the help of many people. We owe debts of gratitude to the interviewees who appear throughout this book for giving so generously of their time as well as the organizations that granted permission for us to use their stories. We especially extend our heartfelt thanks to Peter Less for inviting us into your home and sharing your experiences but, most important, for inspiring us through your service to humanity.

Our thanks to Caitilin Walsh and the American Translators Association for your support of this book. We also thank Professor Barry Slaughter Olsen of the Monterey Institute of International Studies and InterpretAmerica for so generously introducing us to several of the interviewees who appear in these stories. Judy Jenner, your bubbling enthusiasm for our book was contagious, and your friendship to us both is truly appreciated. Thanks also to Rina Ne'eman for reviewing the Hebrew translations included in this book.

To David Crystal, it is both an honor and a delight that a foreword from one of the world's most renowned writers on language graces the pages of our book. Your work has inspired so many to take an interest in language. With this book, we hope to ignite a similar interest in translation and interpreting among readers.

Our sincere appreciation to the many colleagues who helped us with translations and fact-checking for various languages: Wu

Zhijie, Gabriela Marziali de Alfaya, Ali Djebli, Janet Biswas, Thelma Sabim, Konstantin Dranch, Izumi Suzuki, Dagmar Jenner, Judy Jenner, Wawan Eko Yulianto, Kamran Nadeem, Subbanna Varanasi, Mai Tran, Marilyse Benyakar, and Farah Arjang.

Special thanks to the following individuals, who helped us secure interviews with many of the people featured and quoted throughout the book: Shant Apelian, Nadja Blagojevic, Edie Burge, Tammy Cecil, Jason Freidenfelds, Christine Grieve, Kristi Ernsting, Stacy Hamilton, Elyse Heckman, Carolina Janssen, Erin O'Harra, Jodi Olson, Sarah Reed, Krisztina Radosavljevic-Szilagyi, Margaret Sullivan, Anne Taylor, and Lena Zuniga.

We are tremendously grateful to our agent Scott Mendel, who understood, from our very first phone call, why we care so much about translation. To our editor Marian Lizzi and the team at Perigee/Penguin, we cannot thank you enough for recognizing the importance of translation and putting your energy behind this project, which truly represents our lives' passion.

From Nataly Kelly

I sincerely thank my parents, Steven and Linda Fletcher and my husband's parents, Henry and Mary Kelly, as well as Judith Walcott, Darryl Morris, Katrina Kosec, Richard Smith, Marjory Bancroft, Katharine Allen, Heather Rassi, Darci Graves, and Laura Rittmuller for your support and guidance. Helen Kim, thank you for instilling in me an appreciation for other languages and cultures from the time I was just a toddler. Your influence shaped who I am. To my colleagues at Common Sense Advisory—Tahar Bouhafs, Don DePalma, Melissa Gillespie, Simona Bertozzi, Benjamin Sargent, Rebecca Ray, Vijayalaxmi Hegde, Marc Jeton, Bill Ameral, Anna Abgaryan, and Tuba Aytug—thank you so much for your encouragement. Most of all, I thank my beloved husband, Brian Kelly. Your support and love never fail to sustain me, and you always inspire me to do more. *Fil duine frismad buide lemm díuterc, día tibrinn in mbith mbuide, huile, huile cid díupert.*

From Jost Zetzsche

I would like to thank my wife, Kristen, without whom I would not have a voice.

Chapter1: Saving Lives and Protecting Rights in Translation

1. For more details on the case of Willie Ramirez, see Gail Price-Wise, "Language, Culture, and Medical Tragedy: The Case of Willie Ramirez," *Health Affairs*, November 19, 2008; http://healthaffairs.org/blog/2008/11/19/language-culture-and-medical-tragedy-the-case-of-willie-ramirez.

2. Parkview Community Hospital was fined $50,000 by the California Department of Public Health (CDPH) for failing to provide the patient with proper informed consent, which led to the removal of the healthy kidney. See the full description of the CDPH administrative fine at www.cdph.ca.gov/Pages/NR10-036.aspx.

3. For more information on the costs of not providing medical interpreters, see Leighton Ku and Glenn Flores, "Pay Now or Pay Later: Providing Interpreter Services in Health Care," *Health Affairs* 24, no. 2 (March 2005); http://content.healthaffairs.org/content/24/2/435.full.

4. See Craig Bowron, "A Simple Question Leads to Answers in Medical Mystery," *MinnPost*, February 28, 2008; www.minnpost.com/politics-policy/2008/02/simple-question-leads-answers-medical-mystery.

5. To read the full details of the study, see Ann D. Bagchi, Stacy Dale, Natalya Verbitsky-Savitz, Sky Andrecheck, Kathleen Zavotsky, and Robert Eisenstein, "Examining Effectiveness of Medical Interpreters in Emergency Departments for Spanish-Speaking Patients with Limited English Proficiency: Results of a Randomized Controlled Trial," *Annals of Emergency Medicine* 57, no. 3 (March 2011); the abstract is available at www.annemergmed.com/article/S0196-0644%2810%2900557-3/abstract.

6. To see a graphic that was published in the *New York Times* and traces the discovery of the disease in Mexico, visit www.nytimes.com/imagepages/2009/05/02/health/0502-health-timeline.ready.html?ref=health.

7. The examples from the *Tampa Tribune* can be found at www.amtaweb .org/AMTA2006/AMTA_2006-08-06.pdf.

8. The quotes from the text messages between emergency personnel and translators in Haiti can be found at www.robertmunro.com/research/ Munro_AMTA.pdf.

9. Quotes provided by Rob Munro in an interview the authors conducted in May 2011.

10. The quote from U.S. Marine Clark Craig on the success of Mission 4636 can be found at www.mission4636.org/some-positive-feedback.

11. See Peter Dizekes, "A Champion of Creole," *MITnews*, May 12, 2001; http://web.mit.edu/newsoffice/2011/profile-degraff-0512.html.

12. Some argue that North Korea should not be considered monolingual either because it does occasionally have other languages spoken within its borders. For listings of languages spoken in each country in the world, visit Ethnologue, www.ethnologue.com.

13. See "Language Use and English Speaking Ability: 2000," a U.S. Census Bureau Brief; www.census.gov/prod/2003pubs/c2kbr-29.pdf.

14. The Indigenous Language Institute provides extensive information on North American native languages. See www.ilinative.org/index.html.

15. See Julie Siebens and Tiffany Julian, "Native North American Languages Spoken at Home in the United States and Puerto Rico: 2006–2010," U.S. Census Bureau, December 2011; www.census.gov/prod/2011pubs/acsbr 10-10.pdf.

16. To read the full text of Title VI of the Civil Rights Act, visit www.justice .gov/crt/about/cor/coord/titlevi.php.

17. In 1780, John Adams led an effort to establish an official academy devoted to English, but his effort was opposed because his fellow Founding Fathers viewed the move as incompatible with core democratic principles. In general, establishing a national official language has been viewed as antidemocratic because it would be in conflict with the constitutional guarantee of due process and equal protection. The American Civil Liberties Union has published a paper further detailing such reasons, available at www.aclu.org/immigrants-rights/aclu-backgrounder-english-only -policies-congress.

18. Examples of Title VI violations in the United States related to language access are too numerous to list. A report titled "Language Access in State Courts" from the Brennan Center for Justice showed that the majority of state courts do not guarantee individuals the right to an interpreter despite the fact that this violates federal law. To read the full report, see Laura Abel, "Language Access in State Courts," July 4, 2009; www .brennancenter.org/content/resource/language_access_in_state_courts.

19. See Corine Buscher, "Why the Swiss Accepted Tibetans with Open Arms," *Swissinfo.ch*; www.swissinfo.ch/eng/politics/Why_the_Swiss_accepted_ Tibetans_with_open_arms.html?cid=8643062.

20. See "Dalai Lama Thanks Switzerland for Support," April 9, 2010; www .phayul.com/news/article.aspx?id=27082&t=1.

21. For full listings of refugee populations around the world, visit the UN refugee agency website at www.unhcr.org/pages/49c3646c4d6.html.

22. See Tracy A. Schroepfer, Angela Waltz, Hyunjin Noh, Jacqueline Matloub, and Viluck Kue, "Seeking to Bridge Two Cultures: The Wisconsin Hmong Cancer Experience," *Journal of Cancer Education* 25, no. 4 (2010); www .wicancer.org/uploads/pub_34599.pdf.

23. See Kristin Brown, Gretchen Gailey, Greg Simmons, et al., "Child Rape Suspect Considered Free Man, Local Authorities Say," July 24, 2007; www.foxnews.com/story/0,2933,290603,00.html.

24. See Ronald H. Bayor and Timothy J. Meagher, *The New York Irish* (Baltimore, MD: Johns Hopkins University Press, 1997).

25. See the brief on the 2006 Irish Census data from the Central Statistics Office at www.cso.ie/en/census/census2006reports/census2006principal demographicresults.

26. Quotes provided David McLoughlin in an interview the authors conducted in January 2012.

27. For a lighthearted introduction to the impressive lexicon of Irish swear words, we suggest Colin Murphy and Donal O'Dea, *The Feckin Book of Irish Insults* (Dublin: O'Brien, 2006).

28. See the 1905 book by William Henry Grattan Flood, a *History of Irish Music*. A relevant excerpt is available at www.libraryireland.com/Irish Music/XVII.php.

29. The many different translations of the Universal Declaration of Human Rights are available at www.ohchr.org/EN/UDHR/Pages/SearchByLang .aspx.

30. See Agatha Christie's official record at www.guinnessworldrecords.com/ records-1/most-translated-author.

31. To see an example of how the Romani language is used in one country, the Czech Republic, visit http://romove.radio.cz/en/article/18659.

32. See Ian Hancock, *We Are the Romani People* (Hatfield, UK: University of Hertfordshire Press, 2002).

33. Quotes provided by Debbie Folaron in an interview the authors conducted in November 2011.

34. To see this and other comments from Anne Makepeace, visit www.make peaceproductions.com/Press-WeStillLiveHere/PRESS-WeStillLiveHere -pressrelease-110803.pdf. We interviewed Anne Makepeace in November 2011.

35. See David Crystal, *Language Death* (Cambridge, UK: Cambridge University Press, April 2002). We also recommend the Emmy-nominated documentary film, *The Linguists*, featuring K. David Harrison, the author of *When Languages Die* (New York: Oxford University Press, February 2007).

36. See "Official Languages of Canada," Canadian Charter of Rights and Freedoms, Part I of the Constitution Act, 1982; http://laws-lois.justice .gc.ca/eng/charter/page-2.html.

37. Quotes provided by Donald Barabé in an interview the authors conducted in January 2012.

38. See Statistics Canada, "Inuktitut Has Declined, but Its Use Remains Strong," 2006 Census: Aboriginal Peoples in Canada in 2006: Inuit, Métis and First Nations; www12.statcan.ca/census-recensement/2006/as-sa/97 -558/p9-eng.cfm.

39. See the home page of the Inuit Language Authority at http://langcom .nu.ca/inuit-uqausinginnik-taiguusiliuqtiit-en.

40. Quotes provided by Julia Demcheson in an interview the authors conducted in January 2012.

41. Some linguists, most notably Geoffrey Pullum, have written of a sup-

posed "Eskimo snow hoax," claiming that there are actually not as many words for snow in Eskimo languages as what some might think. The numbers for Eskimo snow terms have indeed been exaggerated by some, as Pullum rightly notes. However, as K. David Harrison points out, "All documented languages show extreme lexical proliferation and specialization for domains that are culturally important." He points out, "Yupik elders list, define, and illustrate ninety-nine specific Yupik words for types of sea ice formations. This prolific lexicon for ice is in no way equivalent to the English set of terms for snow/ice (e.g., sleet, ice pack, etc.), but is vastly more complex, more ancient, more taxonomically structured, more information rich, and more connected to the environment. Lexical richness is at the heart of what makes the work of translators truly difficult, and so vital."

42. See the Royal Commission on Aboriginal Peoples (RCAP), "Report of the Royal Commission on Aboriginal Peoples," 5 vols. (Ottawa: Government of Canada, 1996), p. 163.

Chapter 2: Waging War and Keeping the Peace in Translation

1. Quotes and details provided by Peter Less and his daughter Nettie in an interview the authors conducted in December 2011.

2. A video clip of an interview on YouTube with Peter Less describing his experiences can be found at www.youtube.com/watch?v=8G0q4DhhVYE.

3. For more details of Less's experience as an interpreter at the Nuremberg trials, we recommend reading a profile about him from the International Association of Conference Interpreters, available at www.aiic.net/View Page.cfm/article1277.htm.

4. See also Francesca Gaiba, the *Origins of Simultaneous Interpretation: The Nuremberg Trial* (Ottawa, ON: University of Ottawa Press, August 1998). Gaiba includes brief biographies of each of the Nuremberg interpreters.

5. Details provided by Rajiv Joseph in an interview the authors conducted in December 2011.

6. The sources of the quotations are as follows. Ian Martin, in the *Boston*

Standard: www.bostonstandard.co.uk/news/local/face_to_face_with_an
_afghan_war_lord_1_3357101. Cory Schulz, in the *New York Times*: www
.nytimes.com/2009/09/22/opinion/22foust.html. Nathan Bradley, in *Mc-
Sweeney's*: www.mcsweeneys.net/articles/column-12-who-we-trust. Tim
Hsia in the *New York Times*: http://atwar.blogs.nytimes.com/2009/09/22/
jacob-the-interpreter. Michael Griffin is the author of the forthcoming
book, the *Broken Road: America's War in Afghanistan*, in which he dedi-
cates an entire chapter to military interpreting. He covers, among many
other things, the involvement of military contractors.

7. According to an article in the *Armed Forces Journal* by Lieutenant Colo-
nel Paul T. Darling, available at www.armedforcesjournal.com/2011/
02/5622944.

8. Jesús Baigorri-Jalón gives another spin on interpreters and war, by claiming that "wars have been and—unfortunately—continue to be schools of
interpreters." See "Wars, Languages and the Role(s) of Interpreters" at
http://hal-confremo.archives-ouvertes.fr/docs/00/59/95/99/PDF/BAIG
ORRI_BEIRUT_FINAL.pdf.

9. See the *New York Times* page on interpreters in Iraq, available at http://
topics.nytimes.com/top/news/international/countriesandterritories/
iraq/interpreters/index.html.

10. An op/ed piece from *Newsday* that includes Obama's quote is www.news
day.com/opinion/oped/rubin-will-u-s-honor-vow-to-iraqi-aides-1
.3254773.

11. The full text of the visa program is available at http://travel.state.gov/
visa/immigrants/info/info_3738.html.

12. See the stats on Danish visas for interpreters in the following *Washington
Post* article: www.washingtonpost.com/wp-dyn/content/article/2008/01/
21/AR2008012102170.html.

13. Details on the Canadian visa program for Afghan interpreters are available at www.canadaforvisa.net/immigration-minister-says-550-afghan
-interpreters-will-be-in-canada-in-months.

14. Despite attempts to provide visas for interpreters in Australia, the government was widely criticized in the local media for not doing enough to

find them employment and provide further help. See www.smh.com.au/national/betrayed-jobless-iraqis-in-despair-20110605-1fnjb.html.

15. Daoud Hari, *The Translator: A Tribesman's Memoir of Darfur* (New York: Random House, 2008).

16. Limited support exists for interpreters in conflict zones, even though many such individuals are interpreters for humanitarian aid work. One resource dedicated to helping these kinds of interpreting is InZone, a project of Professor Barbara Moser-Mercer from the University of Geneva started in 2006. For more details on the project, see http://virtual institute.eti.unige.ch/home/index.php?module=content&type=user&func=view&pid=87. Red T (www.red-t.org), another nonprofit organization, also supports interpreters in conflict zones.

17. The translation backlog was exacerbated by the U.S. military's dismissal of many translators because of sexual orientation under the Don't Ask, Don't Tell policy. This issue is addressed in more detail in the book *Unfriendly Fire* by Nathaniel Frank (New York: Thomas Dunne Books, 2009). To see an excerpt from the book in which Frank addresses the warnings of 9/11 that went untranslated, see this story from National Public Radio: www.npr.org/templates/story/story.php?storyId=105441652.

18. See the official Justice Department report detailing the severe nature of America's translation problem at www.justice.gov/oig/reports/FBI/a1002_redacted.pdf.

19. Majd, who is the author of the *Ayatollah Begs to Differ* (New York: Doubleday, 2008), made this observation on the television talk show *Real Time with Bill Mahr*. See the interview on YouTube at about six minutes into the clip: www.youtube.com/watch?v=JywNMOzApBI.

20. To see an example of a job posting for a media analyst position, visit www.translatorscafe.com/cafe/job95168.htm.

21. Translators who worked under the George Washington administration included educator John Tetard, Hebrew scholar Isaac Pinto, and merchant John Pintard. See the website of the Offices of Language Services at the Department of State for more details: http://languageservices.state.gov/content.asp?content_id=270&menu_id=108.

22. Quotes and stats provided by Joseph Mazza in an interview the authors conducted in December 2011.

23. You can see a picture of the button and the embarrassing mistranslation at this site: www.foxnews.com/politics/2009/03/06/clinton-goofs-russian -translation-tells-diplomat-wants-overcharge-ties.

24. Quotes and stats provided by Hossam Fahr in an interview the authors conducted in September 2011.

25. Quotes and stats provided by Harry Obst in an interview the authors conducted in May 2011.

26. For Obst's firsthand account of his incredible career, check out his fascinating memoir, *White House Interpreter: The Art of Interpretation* (Bloomington, IN: AuthorHouse, 2010).

27. You can find the *Time* magazine's "Top 10 Embarrassing Diplomatic Moments" at www.time.com/time/specials/packages/article/0,28804,18802 08_1880218_1880227,00.html.

28. To see the original Kennedy speech, visit www.youtube.com/watch?v =hH6nQhss4Yc.

29. Quotes and stats provided by Olga Cosmidou in an interview the authors conducted in October 2011.

30. Quotes and details provided by Rob Gifford in an interview the authors conducted in December 2011. See also Rob Gifford, *China Road: A Journey into the Future of a Rising Power* (New York: Random House, 2007).

31. For examples of insensitivity among journalists who fail to use interpreters, see Edward Behr, *Has Anyone Here Been Raped and Speaks English?* (London: New English Library, 1985), for which the title says it all.

Chapter 3: Doing Business and Crossing Borders in Translation

1. See Gwen Robinson, "HSBC Tries to 'Do Something' in Private Banking," *Financial Times*, February 10, 2009; http://ftalphaville.ft.com/blog/ 2009/02/10/52264/hsbc-tries-to-do-something-in-private-banking.

2. These stats come from the following IKEA press releases: www.ikea.com/ ms/en_GB/about_ikea/press_room/student_info.html and http://info

.ikea-usa.com/centennial/pdfs/Global-At-A-Glance-Fact-Sheet%20_
March-2011.pdf.

3. See Claire Soares, "IKEA and Loathing: What's in a Product Name?,"
Guardian, March 7, 2008; www.independent.co.uk/news/world/europe/
ikea-and-loathing-whats-in-a-product-name-792774.html.

4. See Paula M. Miller, "Harley Davidson in China," *China Business Review*, January–March 2012; www.chinabusinessreview.com/public/1201/
miller.html.

5. See Rich Barrett, "Rules Hurt Harley-Davidson in China," *Milwau-
kee (WI) Journal Sentinel*, September 27, 2001; www.jsonline.com/
business/130678053.html.

6. To view the crowdsourced Chinese-language version of the *Economist*,
visit Ecocn.org.

7. Information provided by Shi Yi in an interview the authors conducted in
July 2011.

8. See Andrew Baio, "Volunteers Put the Economist into Chinese," *New
York Times*, March 2, 2009; www.nytimes.com/2009/03/02/business/
media/02economist.html.

9. See Nataly Kelly and Robert G. Stewart, "The Language Services Market:
2011," Common Sense Advisory, May 2011; www.commonsenseadvisory
.com/AbstractView.aspx?ArticleID=1426.

10. See Donald A. DePalma, Benjamin B. Sargent, et al., "Can't Read, Won't
Buy: Why Language Matters on Global Websites," Common Sense Advisory, September 2006; www.commonsenseadvisory.com/AbstractView
.aspx?ArticleID=957.

11. See "User Language Preferences Online," Flash Eurobarometer Series,
European Commission, May 2011; http://ec.europa.eu/public_opinion/
flash/fl_313_en.pdf.

12. Quotes and stats provided by Theophannie Theodore in an interview the
authors conducted in January 2012.

13. Quotes provided by Guðmundur Óskarsson in an interview the authors
conducted in January 2012.

14. Quotes provided by Irina Yashkova in an interview the authors conducted in December 2011.

15. For details on the Chinese words for astronaut, see http://history.nasa
    .gov/sp4801-chapter7.pdf.
16. Quotes provided by Erden Kendigelen in an interview the authors con-
    ducted in May 2011.
17. Quotes provided by Izumi Suzuki in an interview the authors conducted
    in December 2011.
18. For the article in the *Chicago Tribune* about Izumi Suzuki, see http://
    articles.chicagotribune.com/1987-03-22/news/8701220295_1_japanese
    -mazda-americans/2.

Chapter 4: Sharing Stories and Spreading Religion in Translation

1. Quotes provided by Linda Asher in an interview the authors conducted
   in November 2011.
2. Quotes provided by Martin de Haan in an interview the authors conducted in September 2011.
3. In the United States, the leading association for literary translators is the
   American Literary Translators Association (ALTA); see www.utdallas
   .edu/alta.
4. For the full study of the Conseil Européen des Associations de Traducteurs Littéraires, see www.ceatl.eu/wp-content/uploads/2010/09/sur
   veyuk.pdf.
5. See Janine Yasovant, "The Mystery of Agatha Christie in Thailand," *Scene
   4 Magazine*, December 2007; www.archives.scene4.com/dec-2007/html/
   janineyasovant1207.html.
6. See the full text of the Berne Convention on Protection of Artistic and
   Literary Works at www.wipo.int/treaties/en/ip/berne/trtdocs_wo001
   .html.
7. See Denys Johnson-Davies and Najib Mahfuz, *Memories in Translation:
   A Life between the Lines of Arabic Literature* (Cairo: American University
   in Cairo Press, 2006).
8. An interview with Denys Johnson-Davies is available at http://arablit

.wordpress.com/2011/05/31/denys-johnson-davies-on-translation-no-he-doesnt-like-it.

9. Quotes provided by Aida Marcuse in an interview the authors conducted in September 2011.

10. For a review from a reader who actually prefers the Spanish translation to the English original, see www.amazon.com/review/RHIXJ8CK1CHZB/ref=cm_cr_pr_perm?ie=UTF8&ASIN=1880507013.

11. To view the many works of the poets translated by the Poetry Translation Centre in their workshops, visit www.poetrytranslation.org.

12. To see more poems written by María Clara Sharupi and to hear her reading them aloud in the Shuar language, visit www.poetrytranslation.org/poets/Maria_Clara_Sharupi_Jua.

13. The full webcast of Charles Simic's talk is available at www.loc.gov/today/cyberlc/feature_wdesc.php?rec=4333.

14. See Sangkeun Kim, *Strange Names of God: The Missionary Translation of the Divine Name and the Chinese Responses to Matteo Ricci's "Shangti" in Late Ming China, 1583–1644* (New York: Peter Lang Publications, 2005).

15. See Jost O. Zetzsche, *The Bible in China: The History of the Union Version or the Culmination of Protestant Missionary Bible Translation in China* (Bonn, Germany: Institut Monumenta Serica, 1999), p. 84.

16. Ibid., pp. 72–84.

17. Ibid., pp. 82–90.

18. Ibid., pp. 26–31.

19. See Robert Hayward, *Saint Jerome's Hebrew Questions on Genesis* (Oxford, UK: Oxford University Press, 1999).

20. For challenging and modern views on religious translation, we recommend Israeli documentary filmmaker Nurith Aviv's Language film trilogy: *Misafa Lesafa* (From Language to Language, 2004), *Langue sacrée, langue parlée* (Sacred Language Spoken Language, 2008), and *Traduire* (Translating, 2011). Together they give a beautiful and multifaceted glance into the history of Hebrew and the meaning of language and translation.

21. Learn more about the project at http://84000.co.

22. For the formidable language-learning requirements for Buddhologists, see Kate Crosby, "What Does Not Get Translated in Buddhist Studies and the Impact of Teaching," in Lynne Long, ed., *Translation and Religion* (Clevedon, UK: Multilingual Matters, 2005).

23. Quotes provided by Tarif Khalidi in an interview the authors conducted in November 2011.

24. Quotes provided by Nazeer Ahmed in an interview the authors conducted in November 2011.

25. Sites that offer translated versions of the Koran alongside the recited Arabic version include http://quran.com and http://listen2quran.com.

26. See Muhammad Bāqir Behbūdī and Colin Turner, "The Translator's Introduction," *The Quran: A New Interpretation* (London: Curzon, 1998).

27. See Ruth Sanders, *German: Biography of a Language* (New York: Oxford University Press, 2010).

Chapter 5: Partaking in Pleasures and Delighting the Senses in Translation

1. The video of the poor couple who renewed their vows sans interpreter in the Maldives is available at www.youtube.com/watch?v=i5H64OOkeXA.

2. For a more detailed discussion of differences in terminology between the Russian and English versions of *Lolita*, especially in terms related to color, see Anna Wierzbicka, "In What Colors Did Nabakov See the World?," in Vivan Cook and Benedetta Bassetti, eds., *Language and Bilingual Cognition* (Brandon, VT: Psychology Press, 2010), pp. 206–210.

3. Quotes provided by Peggy van Mossevelde in an interview the authors conducted in September 2011.

4. To read more about translation at Harlequin, visit www.cjc-online.ca/index.php/journal/article/viewArticle/1034/940.

5. *Kama Sutra* publisher Sir Richard Francis Burton would be classified as a "hyperpolyglot." See *Babel No More* (New York: Free Press, 2012) by Michael Erard, a great book exploring this subject and profiling some of the world's most notable but extreme language learners, both dead and living.

6. A more modern translation of the *Kama Sutra* was carried out by Aditya Haksar, an Indian scholar and translator and published in 2011 by Penguin.

7. See Naohiro Yoshida, "Translator Specialized in Love Letters," *Chicago Tribune*, February 8, 2006; http://articles.chicagotribune.com/2006-02 -08/features/0602080045_1_love-letters-okinawa-translation.

8. More details about Nakama and the love letters he translated are available in his book, 恋文３０年 (*Thirty Years of Love Letters*). Ironically, like many books about translation, his book is available only in its original language (Japanese).

9. For more details about the Census report finding more than fifty million Latinos in the United States, see www.pewhispanic.org/2011/03/24/ hispanics-account-for-more-than-half-of-nations-growth-in-past-decade.

10. Quotes provided by Sergio Moreno, Mónica Delaorra, and Erika Garces-Alarco in an interview the authors conducted in October 2011.

11. See John Connell, *Health and Medical Tourism* (Cambridge, MA: CABI, 2010).

12. Ibid.

13. See Nataly Kelly, "Stick out Your Tongues: Speaking the Language of International Health Care," *Medical Tourism Magazine*, October 2010; www .medicaltourismmag.com/article/stick-out-your-tongues-speaking-the -language-of-international-healthcare.html.

14. Quotes provided by Eleonora Cisneros González in an interview the authors conducted in July 2011.

15. Quotes provided by Sara Radaelli in an interview the authors conducted in July 2011.

16. Quotes provided by Francis Wong in an interview the authors conducted in October 2011.

17. Quotes provided by María Cristina de la Vega in an interview the authors conducted in January 2012.

18. Quotes provided by Juan Motta in an interview the authors conducted in November 2011.

19. Quotes provided by Kirk Anderson in an interview the authors conducted in September 2011.

Chapter 6: Entertaining Fans and Playing to the Crowd in Translation

1. See Ursula Bellugi and Susan Fischer, "A Comparison of Sign Language and Spoken Language," *Cognition* 1 (1972).
2. Details provided by Jack Jason in an interview the authors conducted in July 2011.
3. See Marlee Matlin, *I'll Scream Later* (New York: Gallery Books, 2009).
4. Quotes and other details provided by Irina Kravtsova and Marie-Odile Pinet in an interview the authors conducted in December 2011.
5. Quotes provided by Mark Herman and Ronnie Apter in an interview the authors conducted in September 2011.
6. Quotes and other details provided by Sari Luhtanen in an interview the authors conducted in September 2011.
7. See the thesis by Esko Hellgren, *Translation of Allusions in the Animated Cartoon* The Simpsons, Pro Gradu Thesis, Department of English, University of Helsinki, April 2007; www.snpp.com/other/papers/eh.paper.pdf.
8. Quotes and other details provided by Nora Stevens Heath in an interview the authors conducted in October 2011.
9. Quotes and other details provided by Colin Pine in an interview the authors conducted in October 2011.
10. Quotes and other details provided by Kenji Nimura in an interview the authors conducted in September 2011.
11. Quotes and other details provided by Luciano Monteiro in an interview the authors conducted in September 2011.
12. See the original article at http://communities.washingtontimes.com/neighborhood/tv-den/2011/nov/13/undisputed-winner-pacquiao-marquez-iii-hbos-jerry-.
13. Quotes and other details provided by Jerry Olaya in an interview the authors conducted in January 2012.
14. Quotes and other details provided by Bill Weber in an interview the authors conducted in December 2011.
15. See Nataly Kelly, "Southeast Asia for Language Addicts," *Avantoure,*

August–September 2009; http://62.128.151.219/A1ehey/august-sept09/
resources/5.htm.

Chapter 7: Connecting the World and Advancing Technology in Translation

1. These and other stories of Twitter's role in a wide variety of situations can be found at http://stories.twitter.com.
2. Quotes and other details provided by Laura Gómez in an interview the authors conducted in January 2012.
3. To see a full listing of Wikipedia languages, visit http://meta.wikimedia .org/wiki/List_of_Wikipedias.
4. Quotes and other details provided by Jay Walsh in an interview the authors conducted in November 2011.
5. At http://stats.wikimedia.org/reportcard/#fragment-21, you can find unique Wikipedia visitor data from comScore showing significant increases in Wikipedia's traffic in the global south. Click on the *indexed* tabs to see the fastest-growing areas, the Middle East and Asia.
6. Stats from Ethnologue, available at www.ethnologue.com.
7. Stats from Internet World, available at www.internetworldstats.com/ stats7.htm.
8. Quotes and other details provided by Nico Posner in an interview the authors conducted in January 2012.
9. To get the most current numbers for translated TED talks, visit http:// ted.com/OpenTranslationProject.
10. To see some of the other translators at the top of the TED leader board, visit http://ted.com/translate/translators.
11. Quotes and other details provided by Kristin Windbigler in an interview the authors conducted in November 2011.
12. Quotes and other details provided by Anwar Dafa-Alla in an interview the authors conducted in December 2011. Dafa-Alla has also organized two TEDx events in Khartoum.

13. Quotes and other details provided by Ghassan Haddad in an interview the authors conducted in December 2011.

14. Quotes and other details provided by Nuri Turkoglu in an interview the authors conducted in February 2012.

15. Quotes and other details provided by Adé Oyégbọla in an interview the authors conducted in September 2011.

16. Jost has created Jeromobot, the patron saint of the modern translator, to encourage translators to embrace technology. Visit his YouTube channel at www.youtube.com/user/TranslatorsTraining.

17. Quotes and other details provided by Te Taka Keegan in an interview the authors conducted in December 2011.

18. For more details on the treaty and its translation, see "Making the Treaty of Waitangi" at www.nzhistory.net.nz/politics/treaty/read-the-treaty/drafting-the-treaty.

19. Quotes and other details provided by Carla Hurd in an interview the authors conducted in January 2012.

20. Quotes and other details provided by Franz Och in an interview the authors conducted in August 2011.

21. To see the full video interview with Kurzweil at the *Huffington Post*, visit www.huffingtonpost.com/nataly-kelly/ray-kurzweil-on-translati_b_875745.html.

There are many associations for interpreters, translators, and language service providers throughout the world. Here are some of the largest and most important groups in the United States and Europe:

American Literary Translators Association (www.utdallas.edu/alta)

American Translators Association (www.atanet.org)

Association Internationale des Interprètes de Conférence (http://aiic.net)

The Association of Language Companies (www.alcus.org)

European Council of Literary Translators' Associations (www.ceatl.eu)

European Language Industry Association (www.elia-association.org)

European Legal Interpreters and Translators Association (www.eulita.eu)

European Union of Associations of Translation Companies (www.euatc.org)

Globalization and Localization Association (www.gala-global.org)

International Federation of Translators (www.fit-ift.org)

International Medical Interpreters Association (www.imiaweb.org)

InterpretAmerica (www.interpretamerica.net)

National Association of Judiciary Interpreters and Translators (www.najit.org)

National Council on Interpreting in Health Care (www.ncihc.org)

Registry of Interpreters for the Deaf (www.rid.org)

INDEX

ABOUT THE AUTHORS

AnnMarie Lidman Photography

Nataly Kelly is an adviser in the areas of language services and international business. She is the Chief Research Officer at Common Sense Advisory, an independent market research firm dedicated to language services and technology, located in the Boston area. A former Fulbright scholar in Ecuador, she is a certified court interpreter for Spanish.

Nataly first began working in the language services industry as a telephone interpreter in 1996. As a blogger for the *Huffington Post*, she writes about all things multilingual. A native of Mason City, Illinois, she has formally studied seven languages, has traveled to thirty-six countries, and has obtained higher education on three continents. She currently resides in New Hampshire.

She is the author of *Telephone Interpreting: A Comprehensive Guide to the Profession*, a book about over-the-phone interpretation. Subscribe to her free newsletter for interpreters at www.interprenaut.com. Find her on Twitter as @natalykelly.

Dan Kenagy

Jost Zetzsche is an accredited English-to-German translator, a consultant in the field of localization and translation, and a writer on technical solutions for the translation and localization industry. A native of Hamburg, Germany, Jost earned a PhD in the field of Chinese history and linguistics from the University of Hamburg in 1996.

Jost joined the translation industry in 1997, supervising company operations for a staff of sixty at a localization and technical documentation provider. He has led or participated in localization projects in many major software, web, and documentation environments. In 1999, Jost cofounded International Writers' Group in Oregon, where he lives today.

He is the author of a *Translator's Tool Box: A Computer Primer for Translators*, now in its ninth edition. Subscribe to his free computer-related Tool Box newsletter for translators at www.internationalwriters .com/toolkit. Find him on Twitter as @jeromobot.

To contact the authors or for more information,
visit www.xl8book.com.

To arrange a speaking engagement for Nataly Kelly,
please contact the Penguin Speakers Bureau at
speakersbureau@us.penguingroup.com.